Details After

Death

Navigating the logistics after
a loved one dies.

Details After Death

Death

Navigating the logistics after a loved one dies.

By Mark Colgan CFP

CFP® and Certified Financial Planner™ are trademarks of the Certified Financial Planner Board of Standards, Inc.

Post It® Notes is a registered trademark of the 3M Company.

Publisher's Cataloging-in-Publication Data

Names: Colgan, Mark R.

Title: Details after death : navigating the logistics after a loved one dies / Mark Colgan, C.F.P.

Description: Pittsford, NY : Plan Your Legacy, 2017.

Identifiers: LCCN 2017937250 | ISBN 978-0-692-85412-9 (pbk.)

Subjects: LCSH: Bereavement. | Death care industry. | Finance, Personal--United States--Handbooks, manuals, etc. | Estate planning--United States--Handbooks, manuals, etc. | Survivors' benefits--United States--Handbooks, manuals, etc. | BISAC: SELF-HELP / Death, Grief, Bereavement. | BUSINESS & ECONOMICS / Personal Finance / General.

Classification: LCC HG179 .C66113 2017 (print) | LCC HG179 (ebook) | DDC 332.0240086/54--dc23.

Printed and bound in the United States of America.

Dedication

This book is dedicated to my beloved late wife, Joanne, who, through her life, shared awesome memories with me and, through her death, helped me learn and grow into a better person.

Contents

Acknowledgements

First and foremost, I would like to thank the two people who inspired me to write this book—my late wife, Joanne, and my deceased mother, Bobbi. The courage and kindness Joanne displayed throughout her life was a true motivation for me to embrace life, live it to its fullest and share quality time with people I love. My mother—beyond being an awesome mom—was also a great role model. She always showed a genuine interest in helping others and never asked for recognition, for she knew the simple pleasure from lending a hand was much more rewarding than any pat on the back.

Additionally, I deeply appreciate the input from my financial planning clients who opened their hearts to share their endearing stories of survival. Their heartfelt experiences provided invaluable information and insight to ensure this book strikes a balance between being practical yet personal.

Last but not least, I would like to thank my wife, Kathy. Beyond giving me the opportunity to enjoy life once again, her love and support has inspired me to complete this book.

Preface

As a Certified Financial Planner™ professional, I was inspired to develop this book as a result of my own loss and the overwhelming mountain of administrative responsibilities that came with my first wife's death. I also realized that while grieving, anyone—even a trained professional like myself—has a hard time concentrating.

Through this book, my goal is to help you navigate the financial and paperwork challenges that arise during one of life's most difficult times. While *Details After Death* cannot replace the one-on-one consulting from a professional, I trust it will provide valuable and practical information to ensure your loss won't be compounded by missed opportunities, costly mistakes, and missteps.

What This Book Is About

Whether you're a surviving spouse, partner, child, another family member, or friend, *Details After Death* provides you with valuable information to guide you through the financial and administrative process following a loved one's death. In particular, this book addresses the financial and legal issues that occur within the first six to 12 months after their death. To help you focus on the important issues at the appropriate time, I've organized and titled the chapters of this book to depict this timeline.

The following pages, and especially the checklists and worksheets, give you a quick and easy way to educate and organize yourself during this period of transition. I've also added a glossary to help you understand the technical conversations you may have with attorneys, accountants, and government agencies.

Throughout the book, I also reference websites that will prove valuable to you as you obtain specific information about insurance, benefits and preventing identity theft. These sites are listed in the Additional Resources section at the back of the book.

What's New in This Edition

For starters, the title! *Details After Death,* previously titled *The Survivor Assistance Handbook,* now better reflects its content and purpose.

Additionally, the book has been reorganized and streamlined for ease of use. This includes the clarification of several key points mentioned throughout the book as well as a complete overhaul and a significant addition of content for chapters 10 and 11, the last chapters of the book.

Beyond making the book easier to read, we also updated it so it better addresses the challenges and opportunities of today's lifestyle, including topics such as social media and digital assets. And of course, we made certain the content incorporates current laws.

The Purpose of This Book

This is no time to procrastinate. Despite the grief and possibly even the numbness you might feel right now, you are a survivor. Read on to start taking charge of your life. Once the nitty, gritty details of your loved one's death are under control, you can begin to heal and rebuild your own life.

The loss you've experienced is unique and incomparable to any other. While it seems like there's no handbook, process, friend or family member that could begin to understand what you're going through, opening your heart to the people and organizations around you may help you take steps toward grieving fully and making a better future for yourself. Keep an open mind while letting your precious memories sustain you through this difficult period.

My Own Survivor Experience

My wife, Joanne, and I had an incredible relationship. In addition to having the best friendship anyone could ever ask for, we shared the magic of a loving marriage. I was blessed with a great life.

Even so, Joanne and I experienced the challenges which life so often brings. One of these challenges, as a result of Joanne's congenital heart disease, was that our lifestyle had to be a bit more relaxed than many. The simple things in life—activities like going for a walk or shopping at the mall—often had to take a back seat to her fatigue and need for rest. Still, these minor sacrifices were insignificant in comparison to the good times we shared. Joanne had a wonderful laugh and a way of making sure we made the most of everything. Anyone who knew her was familiar with her contagious laugh.

With time, however, Joanne's challenges escalated as her heart complications progressed. In 2000, after six years of marriage, her condition worsened. When she developed pneumonia, we found ourselves speaking with doctors about heart transplants.

Even though they didn't feel she needed one at the time, we started the application process. The waiting list was two to five years and they thought Joanne might need a new heart within that timeframe. Interestingly, they also stressed that, while her condition was critical over the long term, they felt there was no immediate threat to her life.

The year 2001 was a roller coaster. While the New Year was marked with optimism for recovery and better health, it ended tragically. Toward the end of that summer, just when it seemed Joanne began feeling better, she died suddenly.

On the morning of Tuesday, Sept. 4, after a spontaneous and fun-filled weekend with her family at the lake, Joanne unexpectedly passed away. Fortunately, even though we had no idea her death was imminent, our last moments together were very peaceful. I can vividly remember seeing her sit lakeside in a lawn chair, gently leaning back with her eyes closed, basking in the afternoon sunshine. All the while, she was surrounded by her loving family. The experience taught me to never forget the fragility of life and how important it is to spend your time wisely doing what you love and sharing it with those closest to you.

The hours following Joanne's death were dramatic. Within minutes of her passing, I found myself amid a crowd of emergency medical technicians, firemen, policemen, relatives, neighbors, and the medical examiner. Within hours of her death, I was writing her obituary, selecting her casket, planning the details surrounding her funeral, purchasing a gravesite for both of us and even designing her headstone. Between the time the sun rose and set that day, I had gone from waking up with my wife to beginning the process of burying her.

My life was dramatically changed forever. It went from a wonderful life to one of tremendous, unbearable pain. I walked a path of introspection and carried on an internal debate about my purpose in life.

During this most difficult time, I also had to deal with the mountain of financial details that quickly sprung up. Some might think that for a Certified Financial Planner™ professional like myself, such details would be relatively easy to deal with. But, like you, the press of my emotions left little room for logical and practical thinking.

I remember asking myself, "If this is difficult for me, a professional in this business, how does someone who isn't a financial expert even begin to deal with this?" It was in this discovery process that I decided to channel my energy into helping others by writing this book, speaking to fellow financial advisors at industry conferences, and making a commitment to helping my clients at Montage Wealth Management proactively plan and document meaningful estate plans.

My Message to You

My heart goes out to you in this complicated and sometimes dark chapter of your life, but I want my message to you to be one of great hope. My journey was bumpy at times, and I felt I'd never be happy again. Fortunately, I survived my own transition and have started an exciting new chapter in my life. It's proof you can find happiness despite monumental loss.

May you also channel the energy of your loved one's life into your own so you become empowered and enjoy a future of promise and fulfillment.

I'd love to hear from you. Please feel free to let me know if this information was helpful to you and how I may improve it.

U.S. Mail:

Mark Colgan

179 Sully's Trail, Suite 302

Pittsford, NY 14534

Email: mcolgan@mywisdomwill.com

Phone: 585-419-2270

Web: Visit our website mywisdomwill.com for more information.

Preface

Chapter 1
Take Care of Immediate Concerns

Even while the news of this death is still fresh in your mind, you'll be called upon to contact funeral homes, financial advisors, insurance agents, attorneys, and family members. You'll also have to start making important decisions.

Perhaps you're one of the lucky few, whose loved one detailed not only important information about their financial and benefits history, but also how they wanted to celebrate their life, including funeral arrangements, interment, memorial services, and charitable contributions. If not, you may not know where to start.

In addition to facing a mountain of paperwork, new terminology and important decisions that may affect generations of your family, you may be struggling with grief. Your grief can include an overwhelming amount of emotions, which can make it difficult to concentrate while you digest information about money, property and other details that aren't the first things on your mind and in your heart.

If this is how you feel, you're not alone. Grieving people often have a hard time concentrating. No matter how smart or intellectual you may be, the emotions of grief may dominate and make focusing on mundane tasks close to impossible.

I originally wrote *Details After Death* because, even though I was a Certified Financial Planner™ the emotional toll of losing Joanne impaired my ability to handle all the financial, legal and administrative tasks that sprung up in the aftermath of my wife's death.

People grieving the loss of a loved one, whether they're widows and widowers, parents, or children, are prone to make substantial errors in judgment because their brains aren't firing on all cylinders. With this in mind, I strongly suggest that in any of your meetings with bankers, financial advisors, attorneys, and other advisors, you bring along a trusted friend or relative—one you have empowered to listen, to take notes, and to ask questions on your behalf.

Immediately Following Death

Notify the authorities

If death occurs somewhere other than a hospital or nursing home, call 911 immediately. The police and medical professionals will determine the next step.

Notify important people and institutions

After relatives and friends have been notified, you or someone close to you, should contact the following people:

- Organ bank/hospital (see details below)
- Funeral director and, if applicable, clergy
- Deceased's employer and business associates
- Professional advisors such as their attorney, financial advisor, insurance agent and accountant

3

- Executor/Executrix of the will or estate

Consider organ donation

Check the deceased person's driver's license or look for an organ donor card. Their driver's license may have a note about their organ donation wishes. A separate organ donation card may look something like this:

ORGAN DONOR CARD

I, _____, have
spoken to my family about organ and tissue donation.
I wish to donate the following:

☐ Any needed organs and tissue
☐ Only the following organs and tissue: _____
_____

☐ If my organs cannot be used, I would like to donate my body
   for the purpose of medical research and education

DONOR
SIGNATURE _____ DATE _____

WITNESS _____

Organ and tissue donation from one person can save up to eight lives. Anyone, regardless of age or medical history, can be an organ donor. There is no cost to families or donors for organ or tissue donation.

Organ and tissue donation is supported by most major religions in the United States and is considered a final act of love and generosity toward others. Throughout the entire process, the deceased's body is treated with care, respect, and dignity, and open casket funerals are usually possible for organ, eye, and tissue donors.

To learn more about organ donation, visit www.organdonor.gov.

In the Days Following

Go ahead and use the decedent's car

In some states, the immediate family of the deceased may continue to use their car until the deceased's registration and/or insurance expires. Contact your local department of motor vehicles to verify this.

Keep track of visitors, gifts, donations, flowers and cards received

The days immediately following your loved one's death are often filled with a flurry of activity and a parade of well-wishers. It may be difficult to respond at the time you receive notes, cards, donations and gifts. So, ask a friend or family member to help you keep track. Knowing who sent what will help you later when you do have the time and desire to respond to these acts of kindness.

In addition to your own list, don't forget to keep a guest book at the wake and funeral so you retain a record of who came to pay their respects. You may find yourself referring to this information for many years to come.

Prepare for the memorial service/funeral

Check for any pre-arrangements for funeral and/or burial

While a funeral director will take care of most funeral and burial arrangements, you'll want to check for any possible pre-arranged, written funeral or burial instructions your loved one had recorded.

These wishes may be kept with the will, in a safety deposit box or be on file with an attorney or local funeral home. If your loved one was technically savvy, they may have recorded these details with Internet-based services such as everplans.com or mywisdomwill.com. In some cases, the funeral arrangements may also have been pre-paid.

Be prepared to pay for funeral expenses

Most funeral homes and cemeteries require their expenses to be paid prior to the service. Some will accept a life insurance assignment, but they may charge an added fee for doing so.

Take advantage of Veteran's and other benefits

Veterans, military service members, and their dependents can be buried in a national cemetery for free or possibly receive an allowance toward funeral and burial expenses. Other benefits may include obtaining a free ceremonial American flag, a headstone and/or presidential memorial certificate. For more details, inquire with the National Cemetery Administration.

Other funeral benefits may be available through insurance policies, employers, the Federal

Employee's Retirement System (FERS), or the Civil Service Retirement System (CSRS).

Check airline bereavement fares

Be aware that airline bereavement fares vary from airline to airline, but have been eliminated in most cases (or are more expensive than going online to purchase tickets).

Protect your house against burglary

Funeral services and visitations are often publicly announced online and in local newspapers, increasing your risk of break-in and burglary. Thieves may search these listings and social networking sites, such as Facebook, Twitter and Instagram. It's best to have someone remain in the home, if possible.

If there are items of significant value in the home, consider notifying your local police department of your absence, particularly if the funeral is taking place in another city. You might also consider putting your valuables in a safe deposit box or storing them at a friend's house.

Get the tax deductions you deserve

According to our friends at the IRS, most individuals won't qualify to claim a deduction for funeral expenses unless they were paid for out of the funds of the deceased's estate. Keep in mind that many estates don't actually use this deduction, since most estates are less than the amount that is taxable.

Decide on burial or cremation

If you choose burial:

Check to see if your loved one already owns a burial plot—If they purchased a burial plot in advance, they'll have had a burial plot deed issued to them. Contact the funeral director or designated cemetery to determine whether a copy of the burial plot deed will be required to bury the decedent. Deeds may often be stored in a safe deposit box at your bank or other secure location.

Contact the designated or desired cemetery—If a plot hasn't yet been acquired, consider buying two, side-by-side plots now for you and your loved one. You may also want to buy plots for each member of your family. Too often, people wait to do this and by the time they get back to the cemetery, the adjoining plots have been sold. Also, you might get better pricing if you buy the property in advance of your need for it or buy multiple plots at once. It also must be said that what makes sense today may not tomorrow. The dynamics of life evolve and even those close to you may prefer a burial elsewhere or no burial at all. Balance these perspectives to make an informed decision.

If you choose cremation:

Cremation is chosen much more often than it used to be and is likely to continue to be a viable option. Here are some considerations:

How to arrange for cremation—Cremation arrangements can be made through a funeral director. You'll be asked to select an urn (a container for the ashes) at the same time.

Cremation still allows for traditional services—If you choose cremation, don't overlook the fact that traditional services—including viewing and visitation with the casket present—are still possible.

Decide what to do with the ashes—You may choose to have the ashes placed in an urn, kept in a private location, stored in an above-ground niche at the cemetery or even buried in a cemetery plot. In some cases, more than one urn could be buried in a single cemetery plot, so you might start thinking about what you'd like to do for yourself. Alternatively, some people choose to bury ashes at a gravesite. Scattering of ashes is popular but viewed as illegal by most towns.

Whatever you choose, keep in mind that the ashes can be separated to fulfill more than one desire. Before making any irreversible decisions, discuss the options with close family and friends. If no conclusive decision arises, consider tabling such important decisions until later.

Obtain death certificates

Have the funeral director provide you with as many death certificates as you're likely to need.

They can help you determine how many must be certified vs. copied.

The death certificate is used as proof of death for administering the estate, collecting life insurance, changing bank accounts, transferring titles and deeds, obtaining discounted bereavement airfare for relatives flying into town for the funeral, etc. Make sure to carefully check the information for accuracy and store the certificates in a secure location. Also, be aware that some states charge as much as $150 for one death certificate.

You can also obtain death certificates from the state's department of Health Services, Public Health, Vital Records, Health Statistics or similar office (depending on your state).

In the Next Weeks

Meet with an attorney

You may already have an attorney to work with to process the will and estate. If not, this is the time to find legal representation. Choosing the right attorney is critical. Many attorneys, especially the good ones, don't do a lot of marketing; they attract clients by word-of-mouth. To find these attorneys, you'll have to tap into their network of clients and colleagues. You might, therefore, consider the following search methods:

- **Ask other professionals**—Ask the attorneys and accountants you work with to recommend an estate attorney they know and trust.

- **Ask clients**—Satisfied clients can be a good source of referrals—but exercise caution. Clients aren't always the best judge of a professional's quality of work, especially in complex legal matters. You don't want a bad attorney with a charming personality.

- **Search legal directories**—You can search lawyers.com which has an online version of the Martindale-Hubbell directory by legal specialty and geographic location. If you don't have Internet access, check at your local library.

- **Contact your local Bar Association—** Go to www.findlegalhelp.org and click on your state to find a list of referral sources, such as your state or county bar association.

  Focus on referral sources that meet ABA standards. This means that they operate solely in the public interest and don't charge for referrals.

Consider the attorney's fees

Some attorneys may charge by the hour or a flat fee; others charge a percentage of the value of the estate. In some cases, a paralegal may do much of the paperwork and will have a different billing rate. You should inquire about the division of labor and the related costs.

Check for area of specialization

Martindale Hubbell, the company that publishes a directory of attorneys in the United States, identifies four specialties related to financial planning:

- **Trusts and estates**—This includes estate planning and preparation of wills, trusts, and other planning documents.

- **Wills and probate**—Most attorneys do one or both of these. Transactional attorneys handle the administrative side of probate, while probate litigators represent clients in estate claims.

- **Eldercare**—This rapidly growing area of law specializes in the needs of older people.

- **Family law**—These attorneys handle divorces and all matters relating to children, including adoption, guardianship, child custody and child support. They also do prenuptial agreements.

Meet with an accountant

It's important that, as the surviving spouse, partner or other family, you spend some time with an accountant. There may be tax returns due, estimated taxes to pay or other items that need to be taken care of as the estate is awaiting settlement.

You may even want to consider a joint meeting with the attorney and accountant. It can be well worth the expense in creating clarity, organizing the things that need to be done, and getting things rolling.

Contact the executor/executrix

This person, named in the will, is the one responsible for executing the wishes of the decedent and processing the estate, including the distribution of assets to individuals and charities. The executor will work closely with the attorney and should be contacted immediately.

The executor/executrix of the estate may be you, the surviving spouse/loved one, an adult child or another friend or family member.

Contact the people listed as witnesses in the will

Many wills executed in the last 30 years are "self-proving." This means you don't have to locate the witnesses to prove the will is valid. If you aren't sure if your loved one's will is self-proving, ask your attorney.

If the will isn't self-proving, or if you anticipate a contest of the will, you'll need to locate the individuals who served as witnesses and whose names and signatures appear at the end of the document.

If applicable, file the will and petition

If the deceased's estate is small or if the assets were owned in joint name, then you may not even need to file a will and go through the probate process.

Some states allow an estate to bypass probate if the estate is under a set amount; the assets in such a case are transferred with the use of a small estates affidavit. Although the procedure may vary from state to state, this method of transferring the assets of the deceased will save the heirs time and money over having to file a full-blown probate proceeding.

If everything was jointly-owned or automatically passed to you or others by automatic beneficiary designation, there is no need to administer the estate through probate court. Even if the deceased and his spouse owned their home with rights of survivorship in their deed, then his entire share of the real property transfers to his spouse at his death with no action required in probate court. If the joint owner wants to later sell or mortgage the property, then most often all that will be required will be proof of death of the deceased joint owner.

Let's say that neither of these scenarios applies and you determine that a will must be filed. This must be done in the probate court in the county where the deceased died.

The petition is a formal request to be assigned as the executor and the will proves this. Probate proves that the will is genuine and then distributes the property and other assets according to the terms of the will.

Even if you don't have to probate the will, some states require the person who has custody of the will to file the will with the court to preserve it. This doesn't require opening a probate administration. But it will ensure that if after-discovered property, which would have been subject to probate, is found years after the decedent's death, the will be available to administer that property.

Acquire the contents of the deceased's safety deposit box

If you had a safety deposit box in joint name with your loved one, you may open and empty the contents of the safe deposit box. If the box was in the decedent's name alone, you'll need a death certificate and certificate of appointment from surrogate's court to gain access.

Once at the bank, an officer will accompany you into the vault, point out the location of the box and insert one of the two keys needed to open the box. You'll need to bring the other key which was given to the box owner.

You should decide whether to continue the box rental or terminate it at this time.

In the Months Following

Consider postponing major financial decisions

Recovering from a loved one's death is a dual process. In addition to the emotional toll, you also face financial issues that may have a big impact on your lifestyle. While taking control of your finances is an important step in rebuilding your life, don't rush into anything.

Most financial advisors recommend you not make any major changes or long-term decisions about finances for at least six months to one year after your loved one's death. Perhaps the most common of these major financial decisions is whether or not to sell your home. Such permanent decisions like this one are better made after a period of time has gone by, when you'll be able to think more logically rather than emotionally.

Maintain cash reserves

Cash flow should be your foremost concern at this time since it will have a direct impact on your lifestyle. Set aside sufficient cash for at least one year of ongoing living expenses, especially those new or one-time expenses that will likely need to be satisfied during this extended decision-making period, including attorney's fees and possible estate taxes. There may also be some surprises along the way, so save a bit more than you think you'll need, just in case.

Make a detailed budget

Make a detailed list of your income sources and expenses. For the first year or so, revisit it every three months to adjust either the budget or your living style appropriately.

The following sample worksheet is one you might consider using:

Expense	Amount
Housing	
Mortgage, rent and/or line of credit	
Property and school taxes	
House or renter's insurance	
Internet and phone (not cable TV or cell phones)	
Water, gas & electric	
Maintenance (HOA fees, repairs, lawn, etc.)	
Housing total:	
Transportation	
Loan or lease payments	
Insurance	
Gas	
Maintenance/Other	
Transportation total:	
Food	
Groceries	

Pet food	
Dining out and lunch at work	
Food total:	
Personal Expenses	
Recreation (Club/gym memberships, hobbies, etc.)	
Entertainment (Netflix, cable, movies, theatre, sporting events, etc.)	
Personal (Clothing, health and beauty)	
Childcare/babysitting	
Education: Tuition, loans, rent, etc. (Not 529 savings)	
Cellular phones and tablets	
Travel	
Payments against old credit card balances (not current/routine expenses)	
Personal expenses total:	
Healthcare	
Medical insurance (not paid pre-tax from your paycheck)	
Co-pays, prescriptions, etc.	
Pet healthcare	
Healthcare total:	
Insurance to protect lifestyle	
Life insurance	
Disability and Long Term Care insurance	
Insurance total:	

Gifts and charitable contributions	
Gifts (including birthdays and holidays)	
Charitable contributions	
Gifts and contributions total:	
"Phantom" or other miscellaneous expenses	
Random stuff difficult to account for	
Other expenses	
Other expenses total:	
TOTAL EXPENSES	

Check for unclaimed funds

It's not unusual for people to lose track of various bank accounts, tax refunds, stock dividends, etc. The result is billions of dollars sitting in unclaimed property funds, waiting to be taken by its rightful owners. To see if the deceased, or yourself for that matter, has any unclaimed funds, go to unclaimed.org. The site is run by the National Association of Unclaimed Property Administrators. You can either search on MissingMoney, a multi-state search engine, or connect to your state's individual site where you can search for unclaimed money. Perhaps you'll find a pleasant surprise.

Make Time to Grieve and Celebrate

While all the above concerns should be addressed, it's also imperative you make time to grieve and celebrate the life you had with your loved one. Whether it's through viewing old pictures, writing in a journal, surrounding yourself with family, or writing a poem—listen to your heart and embrace the rituals you deem appropriate.

Below is a poem I wrote the night Joanne died. It was my way of communicating my gratitude and love. Perhaps you, too, may find comfort in this poem or in one you write yourself.

MY DEAR JOANNE

I pray to you tonight with love,
our hearts still as one.
While your touch may not be near,
the company of your soul I hold dear.

Until we meet again,

24

let the heavens surround you with light
and all of the beautiful treasures
to which you claim right.

And as I finish my journey on Earth,
may God give me strength
and you give me hope,
for a new tomorrow I must cope.

You are the sun in my day
and the moon in my night.
You are the inspiration
that brings me life.
I love you forever.

—Mark Colgan

To-Do List

☐ Notify the authorities

☐ Notify important people and professionals

☐ Consider organ donation

☐ Keep track of visitors, gifts and cards received

☐ Check for any pre-arrangements for funeral and/or burial

☐ Check for Veterans or other burial benefits

☐ Decide on cremation or burial

☐ Protect your house against burglary

☐ Obtain death certificates

☐ Arrange to meet with an attorney

☐ Arrange to meet with an accountant

☐ Contact the executor/executrix of the estate

☐ Contact the witnesses listed in the will

☐ Find the will and petition the probate court

☐ Acquire the contents of the safe deposit box

☐ Consider postponing major financial decisions

☐ Maintain adequate cash reserves

☐ Make a detailed monthly budget

☐ Check for unclaimed funds

Notes

Chapter 2
Collect Survivor Benefits

This chapter will help you determine whether you're entitled to certain survivor benefits and, if so, what you can expect and how to apply for them.

Social Security Survivor Benefits

Social Security benefits are paid to surviving spouses, their minor or disabled children, and sometimes other family members. You should contact your nearest Social Security office as soon as possible to find out if you qualify. While the funeral director usually notifies the Social Security Administration, that notification isn't a formal claim for benefits.

Determining decedent's insured status

If you're inquiring about whether you can collect survivor benefits or not, it's important to understand that you don't have to meet the work requirement yourself. Instead, you must be the widow, widower or child of a deceased worker who was *currently insured* or *fully insured*. This "insured status" is a determination of whether there's a benefit to collect or not.

For the decedent to have achieved *currently insured* status, they must have had at least 6 quarters of earnings covered by Social Security withholding during the full 13-quarter period prior to their death.

For the decedent to have achieved *fully insured* status, they must have had up to 40 quarters (10 years) of earnings covered by Social Security, depending on their age at the time of their death. Additionally, if the decedent worked for only one and a half years in the three years just prior to their death, benefits can be paid to their children and spouse who is caring for the children.

The decedent's insured status doesn't affect the amount of the benefit their survivors receive. It's simply a minimum work requirement which must be met before a particular benefit is payable. Once this minimum is met, a benefit amount is computed based on the decedent's average earnings.

Who can collect survivor benefits

Certain relatives of the decedent have the privilege of collecting Social Security survivor benefits, potentially including the widow or widower, divorced widow or widower, unmarried children and/or dependent parents.

Widows and widowers

A widow or widower can receive benefits:

- At full retirement age (full benefits)
- As early as age 60 (reduced benefits)
- At age 50 or older if disabled
- At any age, if she or he takes care of a child of the deceased who is younger than age 16 or disabled

Divorced widows and widowers

A divorced widow or widower can receive benefits:

- At age 60 or older if the marriage to the deceased lasted at least 10 years

- At age 50 or older if disabled and the marriage to the deceased lasted at least 10 years

- At any age, if she or he takes care of a child of the deceased who is younger than age 16 or disabled

Unmarried children

Unmarried children can receive benefits if they are:

- Younger than age 18 (or up to age 19 if they are attending elementary or secondary school full time)

- Any age and were disabled before age 22 and remain disabled

Under certain circumstances, benefits also can be paid to stepchildren, grandchildren, step grandchildren or adopted children.

Dependent parents

Parents age 62 or older who received at least one-half support from the deceased can receive benefits.

Types of Social Security survivor benefits

In this section, we address survivor benefits which are based on the earnings record of the decedent. This shouldn't be confused with spousal benefits, an entirely different set of benefits based on the earnings record of a living spouse. As for survivor benefits, there are two types.

One-time death payment

If the decedent is currently or fully insured, a $255 lump sum is payable to the widow/widower or dependent child generally age 18 or younger who was living with the decedent at the time of death.

Whether or not there was joint residency, this lump sum may still be collected if the widow/widower or children are immediately eligible for monthly benefits. If there is no eligible surviving spouse, the deceased's child (or children) may be eligible to receive the $255 lump sum. You must apply for this payment within two years of the date of death.

Monthly survivor benefit

If the decedent was currently or fully insured and you qualify, you may begin collecting monthly income survivor benefits.

The amount of your benefit is based on the "primary insurance amount" which is calculated by the earnings of the person who died. Essentially, the more the worker paid into Social Security, the greater your benefits will be.

One of the most common scenarios is when death occurs after both spouses have reached "full retirement age." In this situation, the survivor simply receives the greater of their social security benefit or the deceased's benefit. Surviving spouses as young as age 60 are eligible for a reduced benefit. Depending on the survivor's age, they can expect to receive between 71.5%-100% of the decedent's benefit amount. You should also note that, even though the survivor's benefit might step up to a higher amount, their own benefit will stop.

In select situations, maximum family benefits might also apply. There's a limit to the combined benefits survivors and their family members can receive each month. The family maximum is generally 150% to 180% of the deceased worker's benefit. Typically, the family maximum comes up when the decedent was the primary income earner, leaving behind a surviving spouse who is raising children who are also entitled to survivor benefits. It could also be an issue if the survivor is already collecting a government retirement or disability pension.

As you can see, there are several possible scenarios, each with its own associated rules, so it's highly advised that you get more details from www.ssa.gov and consult with a representative of the Social Security Administration.

How to apply for Survivor benefits

If you're not currently receiving benefits from the Social Security Administration, you should apply for survivor's benefits promptly as, in some cases, they aren't retroactive. Even if you're already getting retirement or disability benefits, unless they're on your deceased love one's record, you may still need to apply for survivor's benefits.

When you're ready to begin the process—online, by phone or in person—make your contact as smooth as possible. Don't delay filing your claim just because you don't have all the documents. Be ready to answer the following questions and have as many of the required documents as possible:

- Your name and Social Security number
- Your name at birth (if different)
- The deceased's name, gender, date of birth and Social Security number
- Your date of birth and place of birth (U. S. state or foreign country)
- Your deceased child's date and place of death
- Whether a public or religious record was made of your birth before age 5
- Your citizenship status
- Whether you have used any other Social Security number

- The state or foreign country of the worker's permanent residence at the time of death

- Whether you or anyone else has ever filed for Social Security benefits, Medicare or Supplemental Security Income on your behalf (if so, they will also ask for information on whose Social Security record you applied)

- Whether the deceased ever filed for Social Security benefits, Medicare or Supplemental Security Income (if so, they will also ask for information on whose Social Security record they applied)

- Whether you became unable to work because of illness or injury at any time within the past 14 months (if so, they will also ask you the date you became unable to work)

- Whether the deceased was unable to work because of illness or injury at any time during the 14 months before their death (if so, they will also ask you the date they were unable to work)

- Whether you or the deceased was in active military service before 1968 and, if so, the dates of service and whether you have received or are eligible to receive a pension from a military or federal civilian agency

- Whether you or the deceased worked for the railroad industry

- Whether you or the deceased ever earned Social Security credits under another country's Social Security system

- Whether you qualify for or expect to receive a pension or annuity based on your own employment with the federal government of the United States or one of its states or local subdivisions

- The names, dates of birth (or age) and Social Security numbers (if known) of any of your or the deceased's former spouses

- The dates of each of your marriages and, for marriages that have ended, how and when they ended

- The dates of each of the deceased's marriages and how and when they ended

- The amount of the deceased's earnings in the year of his or her death and the preceding year

- Whether the deceased had earnings in all years since 1978

- Your earnings for this year, last year and estimated earnings for next year

- Whether the deceased had a parent who was dependent on the deceased for half of their support at the time of their death or at the time the deceased became disabled

- Whether you were living with the deceased at the time of their death

- Whether you have any unsatisfied felony warrants for your arrest or unsatisfied federal or state warrants for your arrest for any violations of the conditions of your parole or probation

- The month you want your benefits to begin

For more information, call the Social Security Administration at 800-772-1213 (TTY: 800-325-0778). This number provides you with automated telephone services to get recorded information and conduct some business 24 hours a day. For more personal attention you can also speak to a local Social Security representative. You can find your nearest Social Security office at www.ssa.gov/locator.

Other Government Benefits

If the deceased was employed by the government and you are a potential beneficiary, be sure to check into whether or not you may qualify for Federal Employee's Retirement System (FERS) benefits, Civil Service Retirement System (CSRS) benefits, state government benefits, military personnel benefits, etc. These benefits may provide death payments, burial expenses, pension income, health benefits, education assistance, loans and more.

This is a lot of information, but gathering it in advance will save you time and frustration during the interview.

The Life Insurance Claims Process

Although it may seem a bit awkward to collect life insurance from the death of your loved one, it's a necessary action. Life insurance often provides you with your single biggest financial benefit. Depending on the benefit amount, it may determine whether you have to sell your home, go back to work, or can count on financial security.

The following sources can provide you with information about any life insurance benefits:

- Decedent's paper and electronic records
- Your financial advisor and/or insurance agents
- Decedent's recent and previous employers
- Your employer, for any spousal life insurance
- Lenders for mortgages, personal loans, or credit cards

Many social organizations, professional associations, and unions may also offer group life insurance plans for members that provide special benefits for surviving spouses. For example, if the deceased was a member of a teacher's union, it may be possible they owned a group life insurance policy.

If the decedent owned life insurance, but the policy can't be located or the agent's name is lost, contact the American Council of Life Insurers (Policy Search, ACLI) at 1001 Pennsylvania Avenue, N.W., Washington D.C. 20003 or www.acli.com. They will search all recorded policies for free and provide the information you need to process your claim. As an alternative, MIB, an insurance membership corporation, offers a policy locator service for a fee. For more information about this service, visit MIB's website at www.policylocator.com.

Ways of receiving benefits

After this discovery process, carefully evaluate the different ways you can receive your benefits:

- **Lump sum**—the entire death benefit in one check.

- **Specific income provision**—the life insurance company will pay principal and interest on a predetermined schedule.

- **Life income option**—you are guaranteed income for the duration of your life. The income amount will depend on the policy's death benefit and your age.

- **Interest income option**—the life insurance company will hold the proceeds of the policy and pay the interest earned. If you choose this option, the policy's death benefit will remain intact and be paid to your children or a secondary beneficiary upon your death.

Lastly, take the time now to review and update the beneficiaries named on your life insurance policies (and IRAs), especially if the deceased was one of your beneficiaries.

Next steps in the insurance claim process

For group policies, follow the instructions given to you by the governing organization. For personally owned life insurance, contact the company whose name and address appears on the policy, your insurance agent or call the company's local office.

If you're listed as the beneficiary on the policy, order a claim form and prepare a claim package. Normally, your agent will help you do this; however, if you don't have an agent, here's a sample letter you can use to start the process.

[TODAY'S DATE]

ABC Insurance Company
123 Main Street
Smithville, OH 12345

Re: Policy number [YOUR POLICY NUMBER]

Dear Claims Agent,

I would like to apply for the life insurance benefits on the policy referenced above. Please send me the necessary forms and instructions to expedite this process as efficiently as possible.

Your correspondence can be sent to:

[YOUR NAME]

[YOUR MAILING ADDRESS]

If you have any questions, please contact me at [YOUR PHONE NUMBER].

Sincerely,

[SIGNATURE]

[YOUR NAME]

When you receive the paperwork, you may need:

- A certified copy of the death certificate
- The insurance policy number
- The amount listed as the death benefit or face value
- The decedent's occupation and last day of work
- The decedent's birth certificate (or other birth documentation) and your own birth certificate, depending on how you want the proceeds to be paid

Insurance companies may also request information about the circumstances of the decedent's death, including:

- Attending physician's statement
- Coroner's report
- Police incident report

- The beneficiary's age, address and Social Security number for federal government filings

Tax treatment of insurance proceeds

Life insurance proceeds are generally not considered to be taxable income to the beneficiary. However, in some cases the insurance proceeds could be taxed for estate tax purposes. There are also some other conditions where life insurance could be taxed, for example, life insurance within an IRA or pension plan or a policy that had some kind of transfer for value transaction. In addition, some wills provide that any share of estate tax related to insurance proceeds should be paid from those proceeds. Check with a qualified accountant to determine if your proceeds are taxable.

Regardless of your situation, request IRS Form 712 from the insurance company at the same time the claim for the proceeds is filed. You may need it depending upon the circumstances under which your estate must file an estate tax return. Ask your attorney for more information.

Employee Benefits

Contact current and all former employers of the decedent to collect the full amount of all employee benefits due to you. This is one step that many people often forget to follow through on, but you may be eligible to receive:

- The decedent's unpaid salary
- Accrued vacation and sick pay
- Workers' compensation benefits

Determine Retirement Benefits

A beneficiary can fall into one of the following categories: spouse, non-spouse or entity, such as a trust. Depending upon what type of beneficiary you are, the Internal Revenue Service will often dictate your options. Be sure to talk with a financial advisor and review your options thoroughly.

Furthermore, beneficiaries need to know that, at a certain point, they will have to start taking Required Minimum Distributions (RMD) from inherited IRAs. The intent of these rules is to prevent families from handing down IRA monies from generation to generation and deferring taxes forever. Once an IRA owner dies, the beneficiary rules kick in—and it's only a matter of time before mandatory distributions must begin.

To better understand your distribution options for IRA accounts, please refer to Chapter 7: Understand Your IRA Distribution Options.

Assess Health Insurance Options

If your spouse is the decedent, one of the biggest financial worries you may have is how to maintain your health insurance.

COBRA

If you received health insurance through your spouse's employer and are a widow or widower, you are likely to be eligible for health coverage through COBRA (Consolidated Omnibus Budget Reconciliation Act of 1985). COBRA covers the deceased's enrolled eligible family members for up to 36 months (more than the standard COBRA 18-month period) after their death, as long as your spouse was employed at the time of death and was covered by the company's health insurance plan. Also, in most cases, the dependent spouse must notify the health plan administrator within 60 days after the death of the covered employee.

Survivors must still pay the premiums for the plan, but you won't have to find, qualify for or pay for a new health insurance plan right away.

Under COBRA, you'll be required to pay the full cost of the insurance plus a two percent administrative fee. In cases where the employer was paying a good portion of the monthly premium, the rate you may have to pay under COBRA will likely change.

For COBRA appeals information or notification rights, you should contact the U.S. Department of Labor Pension and Welfare Benefits Administration Division of Technical Assistance and Inquiries, 200 Constitution Ave., NW (Room N-5658), Washington, D.C. 20210 or call 866-487-2365 or (TTY: 877-889-5627).

Affordable Care Act health insurance

At the time of this writing, an individual can also purchase health insurance through the Affordable Care Act of 2010.

This law put in place comprehensive health insurance reforms that allow people who don't have health insurance or don't have adequate coverage to purchase it directly through an insurance marketplace.

Open Enrollment for each year is from Nov. 1 of the prior year to Jan. 31 of the next year. E.g. Open enrollment for 2017 coverage is from Nov. 1, 2016 to Jan. 31, 2017. However, if you've had certain life events, such as losing health insurance coverage, marriage, moving, having a baby or adopting a child, you have up to 60 days after that event to enroll in health insurance coverage. You can also enroll in Medicaid and the Children's Health Insurance Plan at any time of the year.

Losing health coverage due to the death of a family member is included as one of the reason's you qualify for the Special Enrollment Period and can enroll in a health insurance plan, as long as you do so within 60 days of your loss of health insurance.

You can learn more about the health insurance plans available, their costs and other information at healthcare.gov.

Take advantage of Flexible Spending Account benefits

Make sure to ask the decedent's employer if there was a medical flexible spending account (FSA) or reimbursement account for the deceased. An FSA allows for the reimbursement of out-of-pocket health expenses (those not covered by health insurance) from pre-tax dollars deducted from an employee's paycheck. Therefore, an employee's taxable income will be reduced by the amount placed in the account.

If so, make sure you file a claim for any outstanding medical bills incurred by the deceased before the end of the calendar year or this money will be lost.

Flexible spending accounts are "use-it-or-lose-it" plans. This means that amount in the account at the end of the plan year can't be carried over to the next year. In some cases, the plan may provide a grace period of up to 2 ½ months after the end of the plan year. If so, any qualified medical expenses incurred in that period are treated as having occurred in the previous plan year and can be paid from any amounts left in the account at the end of that year. Any monies not properly withdrawn are completely lost as your employer isn't permitted to refund any part of the balance to you.

Check on Health Savings Account balance

Check to see if the decedent had a Health Savings Account (HSA). An HSA is a medical savings account for people enrolled in a high-deductible health plan. Unlike flexible spending accounts, HSA funds roll over and accumulate year to year if they're not spent.

HSA funds can be used to pay for qualified medical expenses at any time, without federal tax liability or penalty. Withdrawals for non-medical expenses are treated similarly to IRA withdrawals, in that they can incur tax penalties if taken before retirement age and tax advantages if withdrawn after.

Collect Veteran's Benefits

The Department of Veterans Affairs (VA) offers certain benefits and services to honor deceased veterans. The benefits include reimbursement of up to $2,000 of burial expenses, a headstone or marker, burial flag, burial in a VA National Cemetery and, for eligible recipients, a Presidential Memorial Certificate. If you forgot to collect these benefits at the time of the burial, there is no time limit on claims for reimbursement of burial expenses for a service-related death. In other cases, claims must be filed within two years of the veteran's burial.

Benefits may also be available for dependents and survivors. A death pension is payable to some surviving spouses and children of deceased wartime veterans.

Additionally, the VA Civilian Health and Medical Program (CHAMPVA) shares the cost of medical services for eligible dependents and survivors of certain veterans. There are no time limits for these benefits.

Whether surviving family members are paid such benefits will depend on a number of factors, including whether the veteran died from causes connected with military service, whether he or she served in war or peacetime and whether the discharge was honorable or not. The surviving family's financial circumstances are also a consideration.

To check on any benefits you may be eligible for, call 800-827-1000, or visit your local Veterans Administration (VA) office. If there is no local VA office, you may contact the Veterans of Foreign Wars or the American Legion, or even the American Red Cross. The VA will need a veteran's claim number (called a "C" number) or a copy of the Certificate of Discharge from military service (DD Form 214), a military service number or branch of service and dates served. In addition, a death certificate, marriage certificate(s) and birth certificates for children may be required.

To-Do List

☐ Look into Social Security benefits

☐ Start the Social Security claims process

☐ Check for and collect other government benefits

☐ Begin life insurance claims process

☐ Collect employee benefits

☐ Determine retirement benefits

☐ Assess health insurance options

☐ Take advantage of flex benefits

☐ Collect Veteran's benefits

☐ _____

☐ _____

☐ _____

☐ _____

☐ _____

☐ _____

☐ _____

☐ _____

☐ _____

Notes

Chapter 3
Get Organized and Sort Through the Paperwork

While it's common to become overwhelmed with the mountain of paperwork from insurance and mortgage companies, creditors and banks, the decedent's employer and many other businesses and individuals, getting a system set up to deal with it all will help you.

Being organized prevents you from missing deadlines or misplacing important documents amidst the upheaval that typically accompanies the loss of a loved one.

Get organized

Resist any temptation to throw away correspondence as a way of simplifying your life.

Initially, it may be difficult to decide what's important and what isn't. With time, you'll gain a better grasp of what's important and what can be discarded.

A relatively simple way to organize all the mail, documentation and paperwork is to start a filing system. Whether you use folders or large manila envelopes in a filing cabinet or piles on the dining room table, retain these documents in a secure place and create a system for easy retrieval.

Consider using folders or piles for each type of correspondence. Use Post-It® Notes or other clear markings to indicate due dates in plain view. In short, pick a system that works for you.

Following is a list of suggested categories and documents for each folder or pile. While this system may take some time to set up, it will provide an efficient way to retain and retrieve important documents.

Some of this organization you can do as information comes in, such as credit card bills and bank statements. Other paperwork and documents will need to be retrieved from your current household filing system.

Estate documents

- Wills, codicils, supporting memoranda
- Trust agreements
- Powers of Attorney
- Powers of Appointment

Life insurance

- Life insurance policies
- Copy of claim forms
- IRS Form 712 (to report life insurance proceeds)

Employer correspondence

- Benefit claim forms
- Paycheck stubs
- Benefit plan statements

Tax information

- Copies of individual tax returns for the past three years
- Receipts for other taxes paid
- Charitable contribution receipts

- Other deductible items

Business-related documents

- Partnership agreements
- Joint venture agreements
- Contracts

Bank correspondence

- Savings account statements and passbook
- Checking account statements, register and canceled checks

Household information and documents

- Property deed
- Homeowner's insurance policy
- Appraisals
- Records and receipts for home improvements

Bills

- List of bills — paid and unpaid

Credit card statements

Automobile papers

- Title and registration
- Automobile insurance policy

Decedent's personal documentation

- Death certificate
- Birth certificate
- Social Security card
- Military papers

Family's documentation

- Birth certificates
- Social Security numbers
- Marriage certificates
- Divorce agreements
- Honorable/dishonorable discharge certificates

Investment information

- Brokerage account statements
- Money market accounts
- Certificates of deposit

- Stock and bond certificates
- Mutual funds and IRAs
- U.S. Savings bonds
- U.S. Treasury securities

All other assets owned by decedent

- Real estate
- Personal property

Get Access to Online Accounts

As we continue to move into a digital world, more and more information is available to us online. We pay bills online, and we receive many bills, including bank and credit card statements, via email and online accounts.

Because of this, in addition to the above documentation, you'll also need to gather information on the decedent's online accounts and how to access them. Their primary email account is the easiest place to start, as that gives you information about many other accounts and can be used to access other accounts.

Start by checking the decedent's computers, tablets and cell phone. If the decedent had a smart phone, they may be automatically logged into their email account which won't require you to input the password. As email is usually accessed regularly, they may also be logged onto their account on their computer.

If you can't access their email account or don't know their password, you can ask their email provider to provide you with access. Google, for instance, will work with immediate family members to access or close the deceased's email account. However, email providers are primarily concerned with keeping account information private and secure, rather than helping you have access to it.

If you can get access to the decedent's email account, don't delete it immediately. They may continue to receive emails about recurring bills, such as Netflix, and receive notifications about online statements from their bank, credit cards and other financial institutions.

If the decedent has opted for electronic statements and bills, see if you can convert those back to paper statements, so that you able to keep track of them more easily.

However, because state and federal laws are unclear on the breadth of laws such as the Computer Fraud and Abuse Act, making it illegal to share passwords or access another person's online account, proceed with caution. While the Department of Justice has little interest in prosecuting bereaved family members trying to access their deceased loved one's electricity statement so they can keep the lights on, if you feel unsure or uncertain, please consult with your attorney.

To-Do List

- ☐ Set up a filing system
- ☐ Collect estate-related documents
- ☐ Collect life insurance policies and claims forms
- ☐ Collect employer benefits paperwork and claims forms
- ☐ Find last three years of tax returns and receipts
- ☐ Collect business-related agreements and contracts
- ☐ Assemble bank statements, canceled checks and register
- ☐ Put together house-related papers
- ☐ Collect paid and unpaid bills and credit card statements
- ☐ Locate automobile title, registration and insurance policy
- ☐ Locate decedent's personal documentation: birth and death certificates, Social Security card and military papers
- ☐ Collect personal documentation from your family
- ☐ Locate investment and other asset documentation

Notes

Chapter 4
Review Assets

Prior to paying any bills or distributing any money, it's a good idea to review all of the assets now available to you. This will give you a better understanding of what you have to work with and what needs to be addressed.

On the surface, the decedent's savings and investments may seem straightforward. However, there may be some complications that aren't obvious. For example, they might have owned bonds with maturity dates, CDs with estate clauses, investment partnerships with cash call provisions and so on. If they owned rental property, it might have created cash flow over the years but, if the decedent didn't take care of the property properly, it may now need significant deferred maintenance.

While it's important to document all the assets, it's equally important to get a basic understanding of what they are, the rights and obligations related to the ownership of them and if they represent a net cash inflow or outflow.

So, given the above possible complications and the possibility that the decedent's attorney may have implemented post-mortem planning techniques, make sure to seek the advice of an attorney prior to exercising any of these action items.

Evaluate Financial Accounts

Get a handle on all of the existing checking, savings, money market or Certificate of Deposit (CD) accounts, held individually or jointly in the decedent's name. If the decedent is your spouse, first get your attorney's approval, then discuss with representatives of each bank the possibility of switching joint accounts to an individual account in your name. If you're not sure which banks must be contacted, check the decedent's previous year's tax return. If a Schedule B was filed with the tax return, you may be able to obtain information about the pertinent institutions as they are often listed in the section titled Interest Income.

Evaluate Options for Retirement Accounts

If your loved one had an Individual Retirement Account (IRA) and you are named as the beneficiary, be sure to carefully explore all of your distribution options. This topic is thoroughly discussed in Chapter 7: Understand Your IRA Distribution Options.

Transfer Stocks, Bonds and Brokerage Accounts

If your attorney authorizes it, contact the financial advisors at each firm to have them transfer jointly-owned securities to you or the surviving owner(s). They may require resending copies of the death certificate before the transfer can be made.

In some cases, your loved one may have stocks held outside of a brokerage firm. While less common nowadays, some people prefer to hold stock certificates on their own rather than with a financial advisor. Should this be the case, you'll need to contact the transfer agent listed on the stock's corresponding statement.

If you aren't sure whether or not the decedent has securities held outside a brokerage account, make a list of all the companies from which they received dividend checks and compare them to the list of securities held in their brokerage account. If you discover that they are, in fact, receiving checks from additional companies, contact each company's investor relations department.

Check on Current Mortgages and Notes Receivable

Check to see if the decedent held any mortgages on residential or commercial property or held notes on automobiles or other personal property which was sold to individuals or businesses. There may also be outstanding personal loans for which payments are due. All of these assets are considered part of the estate. Make sure the monthly payments are directed to the appropriate person or persons as determined by the will or executor of the estate.

If the deceased held debt at JP Morgan Chase and was killed in combat action or died in a combat theater of operations in 2011 or after, they may be granted debt relief through the bank's unique Military Survivor Program. It provides a huge benefit for surviving family members and beneficiaries. For specific criteria and eligibility requirements, call Chase Military Services at 877-469-0110 (TTY: 800-582-0542) or overseas: 1-318-340-3308 (collect).

Check the Title for Real Estate

If your home was held in joint name, the title doesn't necessarily need to be changed. The property may automatically become the property of the surviving owner. If the real estate was in the sole name of the deceased, then the title must be changed to list the beneficiaries' name(s) as the new owner(s). This is done as part of the probate process.

Keep or Cash Out Annuities

Check any fixed or variable deferred annuities held in the decedent's name to determine the amount of the death benefit due you or other survivors. In some instances, beneficiaries may be entitled to an "enhanced death benefit" that is based upon the policy's highest anniversary value or other predetermined formula. Additionally, some annuities have "income riders" that allow beneficiaries to receive a guaranteed stream of income, rather than a lump sum. It's important to understand these potential benefits. Make sure to speak with your financial advisor or insurance agent for details. Also, consult with an accountant or tax professional to consider the tax ramifications when deciding whether to keep or cash out the annuity.

Transfer Ownership of Automobiles, Boats and Vehicles

Remember, by law, a member of the immediate family of the deceased owner may continue to use the vehicle until the registration or insurance expires. Eventually, when it comes time to change ownership of the vehicle you'll need to establish its value—this will dictate your next step.

Refer to Chapter 8: Attend to Personal Affairs for more information about how to go about transferring ownership of vehicles.

Digital Assets

Dealing with digital assets after death is a new phenomenon that still holds a lot of unknowns, in terms of the ability and legality of accessing online accounts and how to assess the value of certain digital assets.

More and more of our life is lived online. We store everything from email and photos to tax information online. However, due to a mix of sometimes contradictory online user agreements, state laws, and federal laws, there is no clear-cut answer as to how to take control of or even get access to the decedent's online accounts. As time passes, more and more states are beginning to tackle the issue and draft legislation to give clear guidelines on dealing with digital assets.

New York, for instance, has proposed legislation that provides the estate executor or administrator access to a decedent's email, social networking and blogging accounts.

Most people's digital assets will have sentimental value, rather than financial value—their online photo albums, emails to relatives and friends or social media posts, for instance. Often, a local copy of these will exist on their computer or smart phone or can be downloaded from social media sites such as Facebook. More guidance on social media is provided in Chapter 8: Attend to Personal Affairs.

However, there are digital assets that do have financial value to consider, such as libraries of digital music, movies and games. Other assets, such as an income-earning website or Internet domain name should also be considered. Should anything like this pertain to you, talk with your attorney for more information.

To-Do List

☐ Evaluate existing financial accounts

☐ Switch joint bank accounts to individual accounts

☐ Transfer jointly-owned securities to beneficiaries

☐ Locate any stock certificates held by decedent

☐ Evaluate retirement accounts

☐ Check on any current mortgages and notes receivable

☐ Locate the title for all real estate holdings

☐ Evaluate whether to keep or cash out annuities

☐ Evaluate digital assets

☐ _____

☐ _____

☐ _____

☐ _____

☐ _____

☐ _____

☐ _____

☐ _____

Notes

Chapter 5
Pay the Bills

Mounting bills may cause you anxiety, but there are definite rules for how and when to pay bills held in the sole name of the decedent. This chapter will help you sort through the pile, pay appropriate bills and conserve the assets of the estate.

First, don't be in a rush to pay off the decedent's bills. And, although you might feel like you're being helpful, you may not want to pay off the decedent's debts from your own funds. The estate is responsible for satisfying the debts of the decedent and the available funds should go first to pay for funeral expenses, then attorneys and, lastly, creditors. In other words, if the estate runs out of money before the creditors (including hospitals) get paid, you may not have to pay them. Bottom line: consult with your attorney before paying any bills.

Pay Funeral Expenses

Funeral expenses may be deductible from the decedent's federal estate tax return, so make sure you keep proof of payment for all the expenses, including those for the funeral director, burial plot, headstone or cremation.

Notify Creditors and Determine Balances Due

Contact all creditors and check for insurance on outstanding loans, mortgages and credit cards. The deceased may have carried life insurance on those borrowings. If there was insurance on any of these installment loans, the entire balance due may be paid off by the policy. See Chapter 6: Process and Manage the Estate for more information.

Terminate Vehicle Leases

In many cases, death is considered "early termination" of the lease contract, which can mean thousands of dollars in penalty fees. Sometimes, however, there is hope. Some leasing companies allow a lease obligation to be forgiven upon the death of the lessee. If the decedent was leasing their vehicle and you don't want to keep it, see if the lease has a death clause. If so, you may be able to get out of the lease at no cost and simply return the vehicle.

Ford Credit, for example, has a program called Peace of Mind, which allows customers who are 62 years of age or older to lease or finance a new vehicle without the worry of creating a future financial burden for their families. Peace of Mind provides options designed to enable a family or estate to adjust in the event a customer should pass away before completing the lease or finance contract—at no extra cost. These options include the opportunity to keep the vehicle or to turn it in and be freed of the remaining contractual obligations.

Similarly, under Mercedes's Customer Bereavement Program, the family can choose to return the leased vehicle within 10 days of death and owe nothing further. If the family decides to keep leasing the vehicle and the new lessee meets credit criteria, no transfer fee is charged.

If you don't discover a death clause, you may still have some protection because the lease remains a liability of the estate, not the survivor, so long as you didn't sign or co-sign the lease.

Terminate Cell Phone Contracts

If you no longer need the decedent's cell phone, see if the contract has a death or buy-out clause. If so, you may be able to terminate the contract without any further obligations or, at the very least, have the disconnect fee waived. If not, the contract obligation remains a liability of the estate, not the survivor, so long as you didn't sign or co-sign the contract.

Transfer Mortgages and Notes Payable

Generally speaking, mortgages and notes payable follow the asset to which they are attached. So, whoever is awarded ownership of the decedent's property will be responsible for satisfying the corresponding mortgage or lien against it. Care must be taken to ensure these are paid in a timely manner. Don't forget to check on any possible mortgage insurance benefits.

Close Online Accounts

If the decedent had accounts with online retailers, or held any web-based subscriptions, you should consider either closing or updating these online accounts with the proper user and billing/shipping information, if you're able to do so under the account's terms of service agreement.

Meet Charitable Pledges

It's an ethical obligation to make good on any outstanding pledges to charities. Review the decedent's checking account for the past two years and look for donations sent to charities. This will help you identify those charities that the decent supported through annual giving programs.

Manage Income Taxes

A surviving spouse may file a joint tax return for the tax year in which the death occurred. However, if the surviving spouse remarried before the end of the year, the filing status of the decedent should be married filing separately.

A surviving spouse with dependent children may be eligible to use Qualifying Widow(er) with Dependent Child as the filing status for two years following the year of death of their spouse. For example, if the spouse died in 2016, and the survivor doesn't remarry, they may be able to use this filing status for both the 2017 and 2018 tax years as well.

This filing status entitles you to use joint return tax rates and the highest standard deduction amount if you don't itemize deductions. This status doesn't entitle you to file a joint return.

The surviving spouse is eligible to file their 2016 tax return as a Qualifying Widow(er) with Dependent Child if they meet all of the following tests:

- The surviving spouse was entitled to file a joint return with their spouse for the year their spouse died. It doesn't matter whether a joint return was actually filed.

- The surviving spouse didn't remarry before the end of the tax year in which the decedent died.

- The spouse has a child, stepchild or adopted child for whom they can claim an exemption. This doesn't include a foster child.

- The surviving spouse paid more than half the cost of keeping up a home that is the main home for themselves and their child for the entire year, except for temporary absences.

Example

John Reed's wife died in 2015. John hasn't remarried. During 2016 and 2017, he continued to keep up a home for himself and his child (for whom he can claim an exemption). For 2015, he was entitled to file a joint return for himself and his deceased wife. In 2016 and 2017, he can file as

Qualifying Widow(er) with Dependent Child. After 2017, he can file as Head of Household, if he qualifies.

The IRS booklet, Publication 559 *Information for Survivors, Executors and Administrators may be helpful.* You can order a copy of this publication by going online to www.irs.gov or by calling the IRS forms distribution center at 800-829-3676. As with all tax matters, it's best to consult with your accountant or tax professional before taking any action.

Pay Estate Taxes

Generally speaking, if a federal estate tax return must be filed, taxes are due within nine months of the date of death. However, there are conditions under which an estate can ask for an extension of time to pay death taxes. In those cases, where the government grants an extension, the estate will pay interest on the amount of unpaid taxes. An attorney or accountant can help you navigate through those waters. If the estate tax isn't paid within nine months and an extension hasn't been granted, you'll owe substantial interest and penalties.

Legislation surrounding estate tax continues to change. As of 2017 legislation, the estate and gift tax limits was at $5,490,000. This means that for a person dying in 2017, no federal estate tax will be imposed if his or her gross estate is less than $5,490,000. While this big number means that most estates won't be taxable, it's important not to assume that any particular estate is not. Because tax laws frequently change, you'll need to contact an accountant or tax attorney to understand your options and determine the most beneficial course of action.

To-Do List

☐ Pay funeral expenses and retain receipts

☐ Consult with your attorney before paying other bills

☐ Notify creditors of the death

☐ Check to see if there was life insurance on any loans, mortgages and credit cards

☐ Terminate vehicle lease and/or see if there was a death clause on the car lease

☐ Cancel cell phone contracts

☐ Transfer mortgages and notes to new owners

☐ Close accounts with online retailers, cancel online subscriptions, etc.

☐ Meet charitable obligations

☐ Determine filing status for income tax returns

☐ File federal estate tax returns within nine months

☐ _____

☐ _____

☐ _____

☐ _____

☐ _____

Notes

Chapter 6
Process and Manage the Estate

Once you have all the assets calculated and the outstanding bills are under control, finalizing the decedent's estate is your next concern.

There are different types of estates, such as those established by a will, or by the probate court if there wasn't a will. There are also living trusts, set up by the decedent before their death, which are addressed at the end of this chapter.

Understand Your Role as Executor

The executor, personal representative or administrator is the person who carries out the responsibility of finalizing the estate. An executor (or executrix) is appointed by the decedent in their will. An administrator is appointed by the probate court if the decedent didn't name an executor, didn't have a will, or the person named in the will isn't able or willing to fulfill the role, and has the same responsibilities as the executor. In many cases, this person is the surviving spouse, but can also be another family member of close family friend.

The executor is responsible for administering and distributing the decedent's property and carrying out the wishes specified in the will. An executor's role varies from state to state. In general, they are charged with listing the assets of the decedent's estate, collecting money owed to it and paying the estate's debts (see Chapter 5: Pay the Bills). Executors are also responsible for disbursing property to the appropriate beneficiaries. A decedent's will may also specifically authorize other responsibilities or powers.

While it's recommended and often common practice to hire an attorney for advice in settling the estate, it's not mandatory. If the estate is small and uncomplicated, it may be possible to handle the estate administration without hiring an attorney. In

New York, for example, estates with assets valued at less than $30,000 that don't contain real estate can be processed through Surrogate's Court for a minimal filing fee of $1.

Gather All Significant Documents

The person managing the decedent's affairs bears the ultimate responsibility for gathering and retaining the decedent's key documents, including:

- The original will and any subsequent, revised wills or codicils

- Trust agreements

- Power of Attorney (POA)

  Note: In some states, certain instructions in a health care power of attorney may need to be carried out after the decedent's death. While most powers of attorney cease to be valid after an individual's death, you may still want to gather those documents and make sure that all institutions know that the agent named in the power of attorney no longer has any legal authority to transact business on behalf of the decedent.

- The decedent's birth certificate

- The decedent's Social Security card
- Check register
- Savings and certificate of deposit account passbooks
- Stock and bond certificates
- Insurance policies
- Real property deeds and titles
- Personal property titles
- Marriage and divorce certificates
- Military papers
- Certified death certificates to file claims for life insurance, survivor benefits and to change the title of property and financial accounts

If you're unable to locate originals or certified copies of marriage or birth certificates, divorce agreements, military service papers or Social Security cards, check with your local Department of Vital Records.

Establish Critical Records

Keep an organized list of all property, income, debts and expenses of the estate. This documentation will prove useful when closing the estate. See Chapter 3: Get Organized for more information.

Inventory the Assets

Make a list of the assets of the estate. This includes all real and personal property as well as the titles and/or deeds for each asset.

Submit the Will to Probate

Probate is the legal process used to prove the validity of a written will. To begin, contact the clerk of the probate court (sometimes also referred to as the Surrogate's Court or Register or Registry of Wills) in the deceased's county for the necessary procedures. (In some cases, the deceased may have lived in one county and the executor in another.) It is important to authorize distribution of property according to the will's specific provisions. If you need to probate the will, you may need to hire an attorney to assist you. It's not necessary to use the same attorney who drafted the will.

Once the will is filed with the probate court, the court will formally appoint the executor named in the will and issue letters testamentary, which authorize the executor to begin settlement procedures. The executor is also responsible for collecting monies owed to the decedent, paying the decedent's debts, managing and distributing the property and submitting a final accounting to the court.

When an individual dies without a will, the process of distributing a decedent's estate is known as estate administration. Each state has laws of descent that dictate the distribution of an estate if there is no valid will. These laws usually provide for the surviving spouse, children or close relatives to receive shares of the estate.

The first step is to have the court issue Letters of Administration authorizing the appointed administrator to settle the estate.

Unfreeze Needed Assets

Until the probate process is completed, bank accounts and other assets may be frozen, safe deposit boxes sealed and other steps taken to protect the interests of heirs and to conserve assets subject to estate taxes and debts. Sometimes, exceptions are made. For example, banks will often allow a surviving spouse to withdraw funds to meet daily living expenses until the estate is settled. Should the bank refuse to allow any assets to be withdrawn, the court can order the release of assets from the estate.

Check Assets Not Subject to Probate

Certain assets aren't subject to probate because they're held in ways that result in the passing of ownership directly to an intended beneficiary upon the death of the owner without going through any probate process.

One of the most common non-probate assets is a home held by spouses jointly with a right of survivorship. The property automatically becomes the sole property of the surviving owner upon the death of the decedent.

Individuals may also own bank or brokerage accounts with a "right of survivorship" or another form of ownership known as "payable on death" or "transfer on death" registration. In states which recognize POD and TOD arrangements, such bank or brokerage accounts will transfer as quickly and easily as if they had been owned with a right of survivorship.

The other widely-owned class of assets that can be transferred at death without probate court involvement are assets such as life insurance and retirement accounts. These assets may pass under the terms of an individual's will, but usually only if the individual names their estate as the beneficiary. Otherwise, life insurance proceeds and monies from retirement accounts will be paid directly to the named beneficiary.

Contact Heirs and Beneficiaries

Follow through to make sure the attorney and/or the court notifies all persons who are named in the will and likely to receive assets from the estate. Retain a list of their names, addresses, birth dates, Social Security numbers and telephone numbers for paperwork and such.

Some state laws require the decedent's personal representative to publish a death notice in their local paper. The death notice serves as a public notice of the estate's probate and enables people who think they have an interest in the estate (such as creditors) to file a claim against the estate within a specified time period.

Establish an Estate Account

When necessary (either required by the court procedural rules or your bank or due to the sheer volume of assets and/or beneficiaries), the executor will open an estate checking account. The estate checking account is used to combine all the decedent's liquid assets and pay the expenses of the estate.

To open an estate checking account, the executor (or your attorney) may need to obtain an Employer Identification number (EIN), similar to an individual Social Security number. An EIN can only be obtained through the IRS. There's no fee for an EIN and the online application is simple. Go to https://www.irs.gov/businesses/small-businesses-self-employed/apply-for-an-employer-identification-number-ein-online or go to www.irs.gov and search for "EIN." Be careful of third parties who offer to do this for you for free or a nominal a fee. Alternatively, you can call the IRS. Either way, before obtaining an EIN, you should consult your attorney.

Ensure that Property is Properly Insured

Insurance policies that protect the real and personal property held by the estate, including fire, theft, casualty and collision insurance, should be maintained and even improved if necessary. Be sure to notify the various insurance carriers of any changes in coverage. Furthermore, depending on state probate procedures, the executor or administrator may be required to obtain a bond before Letters Testamentary/Administration are issued.

Take Caution When Changing Names on Accounts

Before making any name changes on accounts or claiming assets by beneficiary designation, be sure to check with your attorney, as your own estate plan may be adversely affected. A simple name change or even cashing a check payable in joint name or solely to the decedent can abolish the opportunity for certain post-mortem plans, such as the process of disclaiming assets.

If it's appropriate to change the names on bank accounts, mutual funds, stock, and other financial accounts, bring a copy of the death certificate to each financial institution. Stocks or bonds bequeathed to particular people or entities by the decedent's will must be re-registered in the beneficiaries' names.

The title to real estate may also need to be updated to reflect the change in ownership.

Collect Outstanding Receivables

All debts owed to the decedent or the estate may be collected now or may need to have payments redirected to the estate. Either way, these are among the assets that comprise the estate.

Collect unpaid receivables such as salary, insurance and employee benefits. Review the deceased's personal records to ensure that the estate receives all benefits due from his or her employer and any insurance companies. Contact the benefits office of both current and past employers for more information. See Chapter 2: Collect Survivor Benefits for more information.

Value the Assets

One reason to value the estate is if it's anticipated to be over the estate tax exemption, which varies from state to state. The federal exemption in 2017 was $5.49 million per individual ($10.98 million for a married couple). That means if an individual leaves more than $5.49 million to heirs, they will likely owe federal estate tax.

Regardless of the estate size, if the estate has multiple beneficiaries, then the estate and its contents should be appraised as of the date of death (or alternative date). This way it can be divvied up according to the deceased's wishes.

While valuations are commonly done as of the date of death, you might also try to project the value of such assets in the future; say six to 12 months from that date. Highly collectible items, such as sports memorabilia, artwork and other possessions, may naturally increase in value over time or may have their value tied to a key event such as a sports record or the death of the artist. Anticipating any change to the value of each item—either higher or lower—will help you make better, more informed decisions. For the more valuable or unique possessions, you may consider hiring an appraiser to value the item for public sale.

If there are a tremendous number of items in the collection, the family or beneficiaries may consider donating the entire collection to a museum or not-for-profit organization. You could also consider holding an auction or estate sale or trying your hand at an online auction. Online auction sites, such as eBay, often require a photo, brief description and a minimum price you'd be willing to accept. Once the sale has been made, you're responsible for packing and shipping the item to the buyer. If you're reluctant to handle the online auction yourself, you should consider hiring a third-party asset liquidator. They are often very helpful and a minimal cost. At most, be prepared to pay 30 to 50 percent of the final purchase price as a commission.

Notify Creditors and Pay Bills

Notify all creditors in writing of the decedent's passing. Prior to paying outstanding debts, consult an attorney since only those debts incurred by the decedent alone are considered debts of the estate.

In cases where there are no probate assets, the estate is said to be insolvent; therefore any outstanding debts may not be able to be satisfied. Furthermore, families have no personal responsibilities for the decedent's debts. Keep in mind that paying debts, such as funeral expenses, attorney's fees, estate administration expenses and various taxes, are given priority by the state.

Also note that for those decedents living in a community property state, a spouse is considered liable for any marital debt, even if the debt were solely incurred by the decedent. Consult an attorney for clarification on these issues and before paying any debts.

Determine Federal and State *Estate Tax* Liability

Calculate the total value of the gross estate and compare it to the current IRS exemption. Note that the gross estate is different than the probate estate. Often, the gross estate will include life insurance proceeds even though they are payable directly to beneficiaries, other assets with designated beneficiaries and jointly-owned property with a right of survivorship. Note that some states have inheritance tax paid not by the estate but by the recipient of estate assets.

File Federal and State Estate Tax Returns

If the gross estate is larger than the current exemption, a federal estate tax return must be filed *within nine months after decedent's death*. The IRS requires the executor or administrator of the estate to file Federal Estate Tax Form 706. If you need additional time to complete the estate tax return, you can file Form 4768 on or before the due date requesting a six-month extension of time to file the return.

Note: The extension only extends the time to file the return, not the time to pay any estate tax if there is tax due.

Also, ask your attorney or tax preparer if there is a state filing requirement that must also be fulfilled. Each state has its own timeline and forms.

Determine Federal and State *Estate Income Tax* Liability

This is different from the overall estate tax. The estate can earn income, which must also have taxes paid on it. Gross income includes dividends, interest, rents, royalties, capital gains and income from businesses, partnerships, trusts and other sources. If the estate has a gross income of $600 or more during a taxable year, the IRS requires the executor or administrator to file form 1041, U.S. Income Tax Return for Estates and Trusts. This return would segregate income earned before the date of death, and income earned after the date of death. Again, ask your attorney or tax preparer if there is a state requirement also.

Distribute Assets

Consult with appropriate heirs and beneficiaries about the orderly distribution of estate assets. Generally, executors may not distribute the estate assets until after the period for creditors to make claims expires, which can be as long as one year after the death.

Be Aware of Disclaimers

Consider possible disclaimers of beneficial or joint interests by the surviving spouse or other beneficiaries. Some beneficiaries may disclaim amounts that they may be due to receive from the estate. This means that they refuse to accept the gift for a variety of reasons. When a beneficiary disclaims a gift, it goes to the next contingent beneficiary. This can be done to avoid credit claims, taxes or for other reasons.

This option should be considered early in the process to preserve the beneficiary's ability to disclaim.

Prepare and Distribute a Final Report to the Beneficiaries

The executor needs to create an account of their actions (assets collected and debts and expenses paid) and then ask the beneficiaries to release them from any liability to them. As executor, it helps to know about this up-front because you may want to be organized in your recordkeeping from the start of the process.

Processing a Living Trust

If the deceased had a Living Trust, the estate settlement will be different from that of someone who had a traditional will. A Living Trust, properly called a revocable inter vivos trust, is often used in conjunction with a will to avoid either probate in the event of death or to establish guardianship in the event of incapacitation.

At the death of the grantor—the person who funded the trust—the Living Trust becomes irrevocable and the named assets are distributed according to the terms of the trust. Title transfers upon death generally are easier with trust assets than assets titled in the decedent's name alone, since typically the survivor simply needs to produce a copy of the death certificate and trust document to transfer property. Thus, in many cases, distribution of assets from a trust don't require court supervision (i.e. no probate). An exception would be if the decedent had a "pour-over" provision in the will directing any assets that are not titled to the trust be put into the trust at his or her death. These assets will still be subject to probate and directed to the trust by a decedent's will.

Whether probated or not, assets of the Living Trust are still included in the value of the estate for purposes of estate income and inheritance tax.

Nonetheless, trusts are an excellent tool for proper management and distribution of assets. In addition, trusts usually don't become a "public document," thus providing privacy to your family.

The following checklist found in this chapter may not cover every responsibility. To properly complete the entire estate process, the executor and survivor should always work closely with an attorney.

To-Do List

☐ Ensure an executor or administrator is named

☐ Gather all significant documents of the decedent

☐ Keep an organized list of all property, income, debts and expenses of the estate

☐ Inventory the estate's assets

☐ Contact the clerk of the probate court to process the estate

☐ Obtain a bond before Letters Testamentary or Administration are issued (if needed)

☐ Unfreeze needed assets

☐ Contact all heirs and beneficiaries

☐ Obtain an Employer Identification Number (EIN) and establish a bank account for the estate (if needed)

☐ Ensure that all real and personal property owned by the estate is fully insured

☐ Collect all debts owed to the estate or have payments redirected to the estate

☐ Inventory and value the high-ticket items and make a decision whether to liquidate and when

☐ Notify all known creditors in writing and place a death notice to see if any additional creditors come forward

☐ File state and federal tax returns with nine months

☐ Distribute assets, ensuring there are adequate funds retained to cover taxes or closing costs

☐ Process the Living Trust, if applicable

☐ _____

☐ _____

☐ _____

☐ _____

☐ _____

☐ _____

☐ _____

☐ _____

☐ _____

☐ _____

☐ _____

☐ _____

☐ _____

☐ _____

Notes

Chapter 7
Understand Your IRA Distribution Options

This chapter is dedicated to the complexities of today's IRA accounts and is intended to provide you with guidelines for understanding your beneficiary status, eligibility and distribution options. For more information, go to www.irs.gov or order IRS Publication 575 or, better yet, seek the counsel of a Certified Financial Planner™ professional or Certified Public Accountant. Structuring your retirement benefits properly is critical, as it will directly affect your lifestyle.

Deciding what to do with an inherited IRA is among the most important and complex decisions you'll face. After all, choosing the right strategy can significantly impact the amount of income tax the beneficiary is liable for. So, let's carefully review the options you'll want to ponder.

Disclaiming an IRA

If you don't need all or some of these assets and you'd like a younger beneficiary to be able to maximize the potential for tax-deferred growth by stretching distributions out over their lifetime, you may wish to disclaim all or part of your IRA inheritance.

A disclaimer is an irrevocable decision to give up your right to inherit the IRA assets. If you want to take advantage of this option, you must disclaim the assets before you've actually taken possession of them and do so within nine months of the IRA owner's death.

Inheriting an IRA

If you choose to inherit the IRA assets, you can either become the owner (if you're also the decedent's spouse) or transfer the decedent's IRA assets into an IRA Beneficiary Distribution Account (IRA-BDA). Then you must carefully review your distribution options and elect the method that best meets your needs.

Note that the description of an IRA Beneficiary Distribution Account can vary from one company to another. Some custodians call them "Inherited IRAs" or "Beneficiary IRAs."

Become the IRA owner

If you are the surviving spouse, you can become the owner of the IRA and avoid the post-death minimum distribution rules completely and defer any distributions until after reaching age 70 ½. If you are younger than the deceased IRA owner, this choice can be advantageous.

If you haven't yet reached age 70 ½, but your spouse had, it enables you to stretch out the tax deferral of IRA assets by delaying required minimum distributions (RMD) until you reach the age of 70 ½. Taking ownership also gives you the opportunity to name another beneficiary, which means you can also stretch out tax deferral for another generation. Incidentally, naming a younger beneficiary can also reduce your required minimum distributions because you can base them on the joint life expectancy with the new beneficiary. The election to treat an inherited IRA as your own can be made by filing an election on a form supplied by the IRA trustee or custodian, by simply not taking required distributions, or by making a contribution to the IRA.

All this being said, you should check with an eldercare attorney prior to becoming the new owner of the deceased's IRA, as this action may result in unintended circumstances with regards to protecting income if you apply to collect Medicaid benefits.

Transfer assets to an IRA-BDA

While it's nice to have the option of treating yourself as the owner, it may not always be the best choice. If you were older than your spouse, and your spouse died before the age of 70 ½, transferring the decedent's IRA assets into an IRA Beneficiary Distribution Account (IRA-BDA) would be more advantageous since this option would allow you to delay taking the required minimum distributions.

This is also an excellent option if you are younger than the age of 59 ½ and you need to supplement your income. Any distributions would receive a special exception for death and not be subject to a 10 percent federal income tax penalty.

Distributing the IRA

Your distribution options generally depend on whether the IRA owner died before or after April 1 of the year following the year in which he or she turned age 70 1/2. That's when the owner would have been required to start taking minimum distributions from the account. We'll refer to that date as the "required beginning distribution date."

Your options also vary depending on what type of beneficiary you are. Generally, a beneficiary will fall into one of these two categories: individuals (either spouse or non-spouse) or estate.

Distribution Options for Individuals

Whether you're the spouse or a non-spouse beneficiary, the distribution options are the same.

If the IRA owner died *after* the required beginning distribution date:

Take a Lump-Sum Distribution

You can elect to receive the entire balance immediately in a total distribution. However, your distribution will be taxed as ordinary income in the year the distribution is taken. So, unless you truly need the money immediately, it might be better to leave it in the IRA as long as possible, defer taxation and prolong the period of tax-deferred growth.

Spread Out Distributions Over the Longest Life

If the IRA owner had already begun to receive required minimum distributions, the remaining distributions must be paid out for the longer of your single life expectancy or the IRA owner's life expectancy as determined by the IRS. The decedent's last distribution must be taken by December 31 in the year of death. The beneficiary's first distribution must be taken by December 31 of the following year and each succeeding year.

If the IRA owner died before the required beginning distribution date:

Take a Lump-Sum Distribution

You can elect to receive the entire balance immediately. However, your distribution will be taxed as ordinary income in the year the distribution is taken. So, unless you really need the money immediately, it's generally better to leave it in the IRA as long as possible, defer taxation and prolong the period of tax-deferred growth.

Spread Out Distributions Over Your Life

If the decedent had not yet started taking required minimum distributions, these must be paid out over your single life expectancy. If you elect to take this option, it's vital you take the initial distribution by the end of the year following the year of the IRA owner's death. If no election is made, you may be required to take distributions using the five-year rule as described below.

Defer Distributions Over Five Years

You must withdraw the entire balance by December 31 of the year which marks the fifth anniversary of the IRA owner's death.

Distributions may be made at any time during the five-year period in order to spread out the income tax liability.

Distribution options for the estate

If the IRA owner didn't name a person or his estate as beneficiary, there is little room for distribution planning.

If the IRA owner died on or after the required beginning date, the balance must be distributed over the IRA owner's single life expectancy, reduced by one for each year since the year of death.

On the other hand, if the IRA owner died before the required beginning date, the balance must be distributed by the end of the fifth year following the year of the owner's death.

Example

The owner died in 2015 at the age of 80. The owner's traditional IRA went to his estate. The account balance at the end of 2015 was $100,000. In 2016, the required minimum distribution was $10,870 ($100,000 ÷ 9.2). (9.2 is the owner's life expectancy at the time of death, 10.2, reduced by one year.) If the owner had died in 2015 at the age of 70, the entire account would have to be distributed by the end of 2020.

Inheriting a Roth IRA

If a Roth IRA owner dies, the minimum distribution rules that apply to traditional IRAs also apply to Roth IRAs as though the Roth IRA owner died before his or her required beginning date.

If you are a non-spousal beneficiary, you must take distributions either by the end of the year marking the fifth anniversary of the account owner's death or over your own life expectancy, starting no later than December 31 of the year following death.

Distributions will be income tax-free at the time of withdrawal as long as the original owner of the Roth IRA met the requirements for qualified distributions. Distributions won't be subject to the 10 percent early withdrawal penalty.

If you are a spousal beneficiary, you can keep the Roth IRA and delay distributions until the decedent would have reached the age of 70 ½, or treat the Roth IRA as your own and avoid the post-death minimum distribution rules completely. Taking ownership also gives you the opportunity to contribute additional retirement money to the account.

Inheriting a Qualified Retirement Plan

If you're inheriting assets from the decedent's qualified retirement plan such as a 401k or 403b plan, the distribution options may be entirely different. Some qualified retirement plans force distributions to the beneficiaries all at once. This can present issues given the fact that the beneficiary must pay income tax on the amount received.

Make sure you review the plan distribution options with plan administrator at the decedent's place of employment. Remember to check in with past employers to see if you're eligible to receive monies from all funded retirement plans.

To-Do List

☐ Decide whether to disclaim or inherit the IRA

☐ Determine which kind of IRA the decedent had

☐ If you are the surviving spouse, decide whether to become the IRA owner or transfer assets to the IRA-BDA

☐ Decide how to take distributions

☐ _____

☐ _____

☐ _____

☐ _____

☐ _____

☐ _____

☐ _____

☐ _____

☐ _____

☐ _____

☐ _____

☐ _____

☐ _____

☐ _____

Notes

Chapter 8
Attend to Personal Affairs

Tending to your deceased loved one's personal affairs can be quite emotional. There's something about the finality of these simple tasks that makes them daunting. With that in mind, you may want to delegate some of the following tasks to trusted friends or family.

Decide What to Do with Personal Belongings

After sorting through their personal possessions and distributing meaningful items to family and friends, it's time to look at other avenues for putting your loved one's remaining possessions to good use.

Start by sorting items into three piles: items you want to keep, items you can let go of, and items you're not yet sure what to do with. Then, put away the items you wish to keep, donate or sell the items you can let go of and set aside the remaining pile for later. Repeat this process if necessary.

One of the nicest ways to honor your loved one's life is to donate their belongings so they can make a difference for others. Coats, clothes, eyeglasses, shoes and boots, games, vehicles, etc. can all be donated to worthy causes in your community.

Start by choosing charities that your loved one might have had an affinity with and then add others that would have also appealed to them. There are also charities with specific programs that may appeal to you. For example, the Lion's Club is always looking for used eyeglasses to repair and distribute to needy individuals.

Dress for Success (www.DressforSuccess.org) and Career Gear (www.CareerGear.org) are not-for-profit organizations that operate an impressive clothing exchange to help low-income women and men, respectively, suit up for job interviews and be positioned for success. If you're affiliated with a church or temple that has a second-hand store, donation is a wonderful way to support their ongoing community outreach programs. Your local United Way can also give you a comprehensive list of charities in your area.

In order for the beneficiary to receive a tax deduction for the contribution of the deceased's clothing, they must estimate the value of each item. Check for the original sales receipts or credit card receipts, if available, to gauge the value. This is especially important for more expensive items. Refer to IRS Publication 561, Determining the Value of Donated Property. The fair market value is often about 30 percent of the item's original price as long as it has been gently used and is in good condition.

Decide What to Do with Excess Medical Equipment and Supplies

If this death occurred after a long illness, chances are your house is filled with a wide variety of half-empty prescription bottles, unused medical supplies and medical equipment. The longer these items remain in your home, the longer you may be reminded of your loved one's struggle to survive. Consider putting these items to good use by donating them.

Medical equipment can often be donated to your local volunteer ambulance corps or town hall who will provide it to citizens of your town free-of-charge. Local low-cost clinics also often accept medical equipment from individuals, as do the not-for-profit organizations, Med-EQ and MedShare. Learn more about them online at www.med-eq.org and www.medshare.org.

If money is tight, you may also consider selling the equipment you have on eBay or other online auction sites. You'll still be making it possible for someone to purchase the equipment at a lower price.

If you have leftover prescription medicine, you have a few options in disposing of them. World Medical Relief accepts donations of prescription medicine. Learn more at www.worldmedicalrelief.org.

If you decide you'd prefer to dispose of medication, rather than donate it, visit www.dea.gov to look for a Drug Enforcement Agency National Prescription Take-Back Day event or authorized collector. If you can't find one in your area, you can follow these steps from the DEA to dispose of most medicines in your household trash.

1. Mix medicines (don't crush tablets or capsules) with an unpalatable substance such as dirt, kitty litter, or used coffee grounds;

2. Place the mixture in a container such as a sealed plastic bag;

3. Throw the container in your household trash;

4. Scratch out all personal information on the prescription label of your empty pill bottle or empty medicine packaging to make it unreadable, then dispose of the container.

Reduce Solicitors

Receiving mail and phone calls in your loved one's name can be a painful reminder that they're no longer here, especially when it's junk mail and solicitation calls. Here are some ways to reduce the amount of mail, email and phone calls you receive for your deceased loved one.

Reduce unsolicited mail

Founded in 1917, the Direct Marketing Association is the oldest and largest national trade organization serving the direct marketing industry. To remove the decedent's name from mailing lists, magazines, catalogs, newsletters, book/music clubs, etc., visit dmachoice.org and register your deceased loved, free of charge, one on the Deceased Do Not Contact List (DDNC), which all Direct Marketing Association members are required to honor.

When you register a name with the DDNC, that person's name, address, phone number and email address is put in a special do not contact file. A new, updated file is distributed to DMA members every three months. The service is also available to non-members of the DMA so that all marketers may take advantage of this service to eliminate names.

If you'd like to remove your own name, you can also do that through their website through their DMA choice program. If you prefer to do it by mail, send them a letter with the following information and a check for $1, payable to DMA. Include the first and last names for up to three people at the same address (or three variations of your name at the same address), your street address, city, state and zip code, and email address, so they can contact you when your three-year registration period has expired. Sign the letter and mail it to:

DMA Choice
Direct Marketing Association
PO Box 643
Carmel, NY 10512

Stop unsolicited credit card applications

Everyone is used to getting regular solicitations from credit card companies and even pre-approved credit cards from banks and finance companies. There is a very easy way to reduce both and even save some trees in the process. Now you can make a single phone call to 888- 5-OPT-OUT or 888-567-8688, a toll-free number established by the credit reporting industry.

When you call this number, you can request to have your name and address removed from national credit bureau lists that are sold to the credit industry. The three national credit reporting agencies—Experian (formerly TRW), Trans Union, and Equifax—will remove your name for a five-year period from any list provided to others relating to any potential consumer credit transaction that you don't initiate. You'll have to provide some personal information and follow the directions you receive from a pre-recorded message. If you follow these directions, your name should be removed within five business days.

You can also go to:

www.optoutpreescreen.com.

You can even have your name permanently removed by requesting that the credit bureau send you an "election form." This form, when filled out and returned by you, will remove your name and address from credit bureau mailing lists until you notify them that you want to be placed on these lists again.

Reduce phone solicitations

Is there anyone who likes getting unsolicited phone calls?

The federal government's Do Not Call Registry is a free, easy way to reduce the telemarketing calls you get at home. Visit www.donotcall.gov or call 888-382-1222 from the phone number you want to register. You'll get fewer telemarketing calls within 31 days of registering and your phone number will only be removed from the registry if it's disconnected or reassigned, or if you choose to remove it from the registry yourself.

The Do Not Call Registry accepts registrations from both cell phones and land lines. There is no separate registry for cell phones.

If you receive unsolicited phone calls from tele-marketers or non-profits, the most efficient way to get them to stop calling you is to say, "Please put me on your do not call list."

Reduce email solicitations and spam

Whether or not we like it, spam or unwanted email solicitations are something we've all had to learn to deal with. But you can reduce the number of unsolicited emails you and the decedent receive by opting out through the Direct Marketing Association's Email Preference Service. Visit www.dmachoice.org for more information. Adding the decedent to the DMA's Deceased Do Not Contact list should also include email solicitations.

How to Handle Email Accounts

Today, so much communication takes place over the Internet that email addresses have become as significant as U.S. mailing addresses.

You may selectively use the decedent's email address book to determine names of people who should be notified of their death.

Consider keeping their email account open for several months following the death. However, due to unclear federal law in terms of the legality of actually using an email account other than your own, make sure you have your own email account to which you can redirect important correspondence as well as further weed out junk email and undesired web-based solicitations.

How to Handle Social Media Accounts

For many people, social media is a big part of their lives. Facebook, LinkedIn, Twitter, Instagram, Pinterest and other social media sites act as a central hub connecting people with their friends, family, history and memories.

Given their importance, rather than simply deleting your loved one's social media accounts, you might consider making them a legacy account. Facebook for instance now empowers users to assign a legacy contact—someone who can look after your account after you die and who has the option to share a final message on your behalf or provide information about a memorial service, respond to new friend requests, update your profile pictures and download a copy of what you've shared on Facebook. And, according to Facebook, they may add additional capabilities for legacy contacts in the future.

Also, a new company has emerged called Dead Social (www.deadsocial.org). The company is committed to changing the way society thinks about and prepares for death online. They provide a range of online tools and resources worth checking out.

Transfer Vehicle Ownership

If you're going to transfer the ownership of any vehicles owned by the decedent, you must first locate the title for each. If the title is lost, apply for a duplicate title in the name of the deceased. The duplicate title may then be used to transfer vehicle ownership.

In many states, ownership of registered vehicles may automatically be transferred to the surviving spouse or children <u>under</u> age 21. A surviving spouse or child transferring a registration to their own name may receive credit for the unexpired portion of the deceased's registration. Some state governments even allow the survivors to keep the same license plates, however, title and transaction fees still apply.

When there is no will, estate, surviving spouse or surviving minor child, the next of kin may complete the transfer. A copy of the death certificate is required. For more information about the specific process for transferring ownership, contact your local Department of Motor Vehicles.

Change or Cancel Utility Accounts

Utilities include gas, electricity, water/sewer, garbage collection, cable, Internet access, etc. If the decedent's name is on the utility account, contact the company to change or cancel the account. They often don't need proof of death to make this change, but this varies by company.

Redirect Property Taxes

If the decedent and the survivor jointly owned property, the estate will likely transfer the property tax to the survivor.

Modify Home and Auto Insurance

If necessary, contact the appropriate insurers to modify accounts with proper names. Check the mortgage or car title for the name of the insurance company. You may or may not need proof of death to modify the name of the insured.

Change or Cancel Other Accounts

Where there are existing accounts with grocery stores, pharmacies, libraries, discount wholesale stores, department stores, pet stores, hardware stores, office supply stores, bookstores, and electronic toll collection services such as EZ Pass and Sun Pass, contact the appropriate company to cancel any accounts no longer used or update accounts with name of the surviving spouse or child. You usually don't need proof of death to do this.

Complete Decedent's Unfinished Business

If the death was quick or unexpected, it's likely your loved one left unfinished business. It's important for you complete, return, cancel or pick-up any of the various plans or activities in process. On the next page, we've started a list and given you space to add other items.

To-Do List

☐ Donate or sell clothes, eyeglasses and medical equipment and supplies

☐ Contact the DMA to stop unwanted mail and email

☐ Contact the credit reporting industry to stop receiving credit card offers

☐ Register your home and cell phone numbers with the Do Not Call Registry

☐ Decide how to handle social media accounts

☐ Transfer vehicle ownership

☐ Change or cancel utility accounts

☐ Redirect property taxes (if needed)

☐ Modify home and auto insurance policies

☐ Cancel open retail credit card accounts

☐ Cancel or change names on existing loyalty program accounts such as with your grocery store, pharmacy, library, discount wholesale stores, department stores, pet store, hardware store, office supply store, bookstore, etc.

☐ Cancel or change names on electronic toll collection services

☐ Pick up dry cleaning or tailoring, shoes, skis, etc.

☐ Return library books, videos, DVDs, etc.

(Note: Any fines are a debt of the estate.)

- [ ] Return recent purchases that are unused or no longer needed and cancel purchases on layaway
- [ ] Cancel future appointments with doctors, dentists, or other services
- [ ] Cancel vacations or other pre-planned events
- [ ] _____
- [ ] _____
- [ ] _____
- [ ] _____
- [ ] _____
- [ ] _____
- [ ] _____
- [ ] _____
- [ ] _____
- [ ] _____
- [ ] _____
- [ ] _____

Notes

Chapter 9
Avoid Identity Theft

Identity theft occurs when someone obtains and uses your personal information, such as your name or Social Security number, without your knowledge, to commit fraud or theft. The identity thief can use your information to fraudulently apply for credit, file taxes or get medical services.

The 2016 Identity Fraud Study, released by Javelin Strategy & Research, found that $15 billion was stolen from 13.1 million U.S. consumers in 2015, compared with $16 billion and 12.7 million victims a year earlier. In the past six years identity thieves have stolen $112 billion.

While companies usually have security standards and procedures in place to prevent unauthorized access to customer information, you should still take your own precautions. Here are some steps you can take to avoid becoming a victim of identity theft.

Protect Your Personal Information

- In obituaries, don't include the deceased's birth date, place of birth, last job or address.

- Immediately send death certificate copies by certified mail to the three main credit reporting agencies to request a "deceased alert" be placed on the credit report.

- Report the death to the Social Security Administration and the Department of Motor Vehicles.

- Starting the month after death, check the deceased's credit report for suspicious activity at annualcreditreport.com.

- Only give out your Social Security number when absolutely necessary.

- Don't carry your Social Security number in your wallet or write it on notepads or checks.

- Don't respond to unsolicited requests by phone, mail or online, for your personal information, such as your name, birthday, Social Security number or bank account number.

- When you enter your password or PIN number on computers and ATMs, shield the keypad so the information stays private.

- Shred papers such as receipts, credit offers, account statements and expired credit cards to prevent dumpster divers from obtaining your personal information.

- Drop paid bills directly into U.S. Postal mailboxes or at the post office, not in your home mailbox.

- Collect mail promptly and don't leave it sitting in your mailbox. If you're going to be away from home, have someone check and bring in your mail or ask the post office to put it on hold.

- Don't ever sign blank forms.

- Verify beneficiary information on life insurance and retirement accounts on a regular basis.

- Pay attention to your billing cycles and contact the company if your bills or financial statements are late.

- Destroy or blackout the labels on prescription medicine before you discard the container.

- Don't share your health insurance information with anyone who offers free health services or products.

Protect Your Electronic Information

Protect online user IDs and passwords

Create strong passwords, especially for credit, bank and email accounts. Don't use your Social Security number, date of birth, or mother's maiden name as a PIN or password. Instead, think of a special phrase and use the first letter of each word as your password, substituting some numbers for words or letters. For example, "I love to see my grandkids!" could become, "Il2cmGK!"

Also, don't have your web browser store your passwords, as they aren't secure. Anyone with access to your web browser can find them. Alternatively, you might want to consider a secure online password vault such as lastpass.com. These services are incredibly convenient and most experts believe they are extremely secure.

Control access to your computer

Set up a user password on your computer. Remember that your browser history files will automatically record recent web pages visited as well as specific access information. If someone were to have access to your personal computer, they may also have the same access to web accounts previously established by you or the decedent.

Establish more than one email address

Use one email address for personal correspondence with friends and family and another for online transactions. Maybe even a third for finances. This way, you can delete any one specific email address in case you become suspicious or simply get bombarded with unsolicited email or spam.

Use a different password for each email address. Your email passwords should also be unique from your bank account and other financial passwords.

Don't respond to unsolicited emails

Never respond to unsolicited email from banks, credit card companies, online auction or PayPal sites asking you to verify or update personal and account information. Scammers are constantly casting about for people's financial information by luring unsuspecting victims through a technique called phishing.

Phishing is a high-tech scam that uses spam email to trick consumers into disclosing their credit card numbers, bank account information, Social Security numbers, passwords and other sensitive personal information. Consumers who provide their financial information in response to an unsolicited email could be at risk of identity theft.

If a company that claims to have an account with you sends you an email asking you to log on to their website, don't click on the link. Instead, go to the company's website directly and contact them through their customer service link or call the customer service number on your account statement.

Don't overshare online

Be aware of what you post that's publicly available. People can use this information to steal your information and possibly answer the "challenge" security questions on online account. Don't post your Social Security information, address, phone number or account numbers in publicly accessible sites.

Look into your privacy settings on social media sites such as Facebook, and make sure that you know who you're sharing information with.

Dispose of electronics safely

Before you get rid of your, or the decedent's, cell phone or computer, make sure you've removed all the personal information on it. For a computer, use a wipe utility program to erase and overwrite the entire hard drive. For a cell phone, do a factory reset. Then dispose of the electronics at an authorized dealer such as Best Buy.

Protect against hackers

Hackers are people who use their computers to gain unauthorized access to someone else's data. To help avoid your computer from being "hacked" get a network security system (firewall) for your computer and keep your virus and spyware software up-to-date.

Use Wi-Fi carefully

If you log-in to public wireless networks at coffee shops, libraries, airports, hotels or public places, check to make sure that the information you send is protected. If you log into an encrypted website, the information you send to and from that site will be protected. Encrypted websites can be identified by the "https" at the beginning of the web address. Specifically, the "s" in https denotes it is secure.

Protect Your Medical Information

Medical identity theft happens when someone steals your health insurance information and uses your health insurance to get medical care, buy medication or submit fake claims to Medicare in your name. This is why you have to show your ID or driver's license, along with your health insurance card, when you see a new doctor or health care specialist.

To prevent medical identity theft:

- Guard your Social Security, Medicare and health insurance identification numbers. Only give them to your physician or other approved health care providers. In most cases, you don't need to give your Social Security number to health care providers. They use your health insurance subscriber number to bill your insurance.

- Regularly review your explanation of benefits form or Medicare Summary notes to make sure that the claims match the services you've received. Report any questionable charges to your health insurance provider or Medicare.

- Request and review your medical records for inaccuracies and conditions you don't have. This can be a good idea from a medical standpoint too, as mistakes are sometimes made or important information, such as diagnoses or test results, aren't properly conveyed to the patient.

If you suspect you've been the victim of Medicare fraud, contact the U.S. Department of Health and Human Services' Inspector General at 800-447-8477. If you have health insurance other than Medicare, contact your health insurance company.

Monitor Activity on Credit Cards and Bank Accounts

Monitor credit card bills and credit reports for unauthorized transactions. If you're a victim of identify fraud, you'll find purchases or withdrawals you never made on your credit card or debit account. Review your bank and credit card statements carefully as soon as you receive them. Report any unauthorized purchases to the credit card company immediately. Chances are you won't be required to pay for them.

Keep an eye out for automated double billings

Many people now use their credit cards to pay for their satellite TV or cable, EZ Pass, Netflix and other services that have a monthly service charge. As you check your credit card bills, be on the lookout for double billings or the same debit amount to the same service provider appearing twice in one month or one quarter.

Report Fraud Immediately

The first line of defense is to become more aware of identity theft and more aggressive in personally protecting yourself. A 2003 Federal Trade Commission report said 26 percent of all identity theft victims discover the misuse within one week to one month after it begins, but 12 percent take over six months to discover the problem.

The faster you report any incidence of fraud, the faster the bank or credit card company can start to close accounts and clear your name right away. Furthermore, you should request that a fraud alert be placed on your credit report file so the credit bureau must contact you before any new credit can be approved.

To report identity theft, go to identitytheft.gov or call 877-438-4338 (TTY: 866-653-4261) and file a report with the Federal Trade Commission. Once you have an ID theft affidavit from the FTC, you can file a report with your local police department and get a police report. Together, these two documents are your identity theft report, which you can use as you resolve the issue with banks, creditors and any other companies where fraudulent accounts were set up in your name.

Also contact each of the credit reporting agencies to place fraud alerts of freezes on your accounts so no one can apply for credit with your name and Social Security number.

Equifax 888-766-0008 or equifax.com

Experian 888-397-3742 or experian.com

Trans Union 800-680-7289 or transunion.com

Considering Purchasing Fraud Protection

In addition to the precautions mentioned above, you may wish to consider identity fraud protection via a property and casualty insurance carrier or implementing services such as those available through www.identityfraud.com, www.trustedid.com, www.lifelock.com and many others.

Order Copies of Your Credit Report Every Year

Because identity theft has become so rampant, federal law now allows you to obtain a free credit report online, by phone or through the mail every year.

- Request your credit report online at www.annualcreditreport.com.

- Request your credit report by phone. Call 877-322-8228 (toll-free) to request your credit reports by phone. You'll go through a simple verification process and then your reports will be mailed to you.

- Request your credit report by mail. You can request your credit report by mail by filling out a request form and mailing it to:

  Annual Credit Report Request Service
  P.O. Box 105281
  Atlanta, GA 30348-5281

Cancel Any Credit Cards You Don't Use

The more open credit cards you have, the higher your risk of identity theft. So if you have credit cards you haven't used in more than a year, consider cancelling them.

Keep in mind, however, that this may affect your credit rating, which considers your debt usage ratio in its calculation. The more available credit you have that you're not using, the lower your debt usage ratio, which improves your credit score.

Stay Informed

For more information, contact the Federal Trade Commission's ID Theft Hotline at 877-IDTHEFT or 877-438-4338 toll-free or visit www.consumer.gov/idtheft.

The site contains helpful information for consumers and businesses on a variety of topics, including "phishing" scams, telecommunications fraud, Internet fraud, and the theft of printed documents with personal information, as well as protecting employees from identity theft in the workplace.

The site also contains valuable consumer information on the steps to take if and when you find yourself a victim of identity theft.

To-Do List

☐ Remove your Social Security card from your wallet

☐ Use a cross-cut shredder to dispose of credit card offers, credit card checks and personal information

☐ Create strong online passwords, with a combination of letters and numbers

☐ Establish more than one email account

☐ Safely dispose of used cell phones and computers

☐ Install a computer firewall and keep your virus and spyware software up-to-date

☐ Regularly review your explanation of benefits or Medicare Summary

☐ Request and review your medical records

☐ Monitor activity on banks and credit cards and report fraud or identity theft immediately

☐ Order yearly copies of your credit reports

☐ Keep an eye out for double, automated billings on utilities, mortgage and car loans

☐ Consider purchasing fraud protection insurance

☐ Cancel credit cards you don't use

Notes

Chapter 10
Proactive Planning: Formalizing Your Estate Plan and Final Wishes

Now, let's talk about how you can address your material assets, possessions of financial value and your final wishes. My intent here is to explain the basics of estate planning and share some practical tips. However, as you might suspect, estate planning can be complicated. So, in addition to empowering yourself with the following information, be sure to seek the professional counsel of a well-respected estate planning attorney. For suggestions on how to choose a good attorney, refer back to Chapter 1: Take Care of Immediate Concerns.

Draft or Modify Your Will

If your deceased loved one was the first beneficiary to inherit under your will, you must designate a new one. If you die without a properly executed will, that is you die intestate, the courts will determine who the assets will be distributed to. Not ideal.

If most or all of the decedent's property passed to you as a result of rights of survivorship, beneficiary designations, etc., you may want to consult with an estate planning attorney to determine if your estate is sufficiently large enough that it would be advantageous to replace your will with a Living Trust.

Draft Advance Directives

There are two types of advance directives you want to have in place: a living will and a health care power of attorney.

Living will

A living will is an advance directive which presents your wishes for treatment and care when you're not able to make your own decisions. This document is only followed when you have a terminal condition and only deals with life-prolonging procedures.

Health care power of attorney

The second type of advance directive—a health care power of attorney or health care proxy—covers those situations when you can't make treatment decisions for yourself. If you wish, the person to whom you give a health care power of attorney can make any decisions about your health care that you could have made yourself, including life-prolonging measures. Contact your attorney for more information.

Adopt a Durable Power of Attorney

A durable power of attorney authorizes someone else to handle your financial affairs if you are unable to do so. Contact your attorney for more information. You may also want to ask your attorney to include specific language so that your authorized agents are able to deal with your digital assets after your death.

Identify Beneficiaries/Owners When Possible

Where you have the opportunity, consider assigning your assets to individuals by naming them as beneficiaries. You can name beneficiaries to life insurance policies and retirement accounts—both individual retirement accounts (IRAs) and employer sponsored plans. For non-retirement accounts, check to see if a transfer on death (TOD) or payable on death (POD) contract is available. This will allow you to name a beneficiary like you would on an IRA or other type of retirement account. At death, assets with designated beneficiaries will transfer directly to your beneficiaries without going through probate, saving time and attorney's fees. Make sure you check with your attorney before executing any of these techniques.

In some cases, these actions can contradict your existing estate plan.

Consider Changing Individual Accounts into Jointly-Held Accounts

Whenever there are accounts that are jointly held, those assets transfer quickly and easily to the other person named on the account. If you're planning on transferring your cash assets to someone else upon your death, consider adding that person's name to the account at the appropriate time. Once again, check with your attorney, as this action may constitute a gift and contradict with your existing post-mortem planning.

Consider Crafting a New Will or Trust

Your will or trust arranges for who receives the assets in your estate, how they receive them and when. Now that your loved one has passed it is very likely that these "who, how and when" answers have changed, which means you'll need a new will or trust.

Before you meet with your attorney ask yourself these questions:

- Who should manage your financial affairs if you become incapacitated?

- If you die, who should inherit your assets, and in what proportions?

- Is there a charitable organization that you would like to leave money to?

- Who should be responsible for distributing your assets?

- Who should care for your minor children?

- How much is needed for your surviving spouse/partner to maintain his/her lifestyle?

- How much is needed for your children's care and education?

Although it may be difficult to address these matters in the midst of grief, you can surely appreciate why this is such a huge priority.

Pre-Arrange Your Funeral

Recently, I attended a pre-planned funeral. Not only had my dear friend purchased his casket and burial plot, he also planned every detail of his funeral. He picked the person to deliver the eulogy and identified the songs, poems and readings for the service. It was gratifying to know that he was re-membered in a way that truly reflected his beliefs, his tastes and his life.

You may wish to include your family in this process. After all, they'll be the ones directly af-fected and emotionally touched by the service. You should also let them know they're welcome to change the plans if it means they'll better represent everybody's wishes at the time of your death. Also keep in mind that it's prudent to review these plans every two to four years so they reflect your current desires at the time of your death.

Another reason to take control of your funeral arrangements is to ease the burden carried by your survivors and close friends. A typical funeral can cost between $7,000 and $12,000. If you don't make these major purchasing decisions in advance, your family will be asked to make them for you during a time of grief. You may have experienced this recently yourself. Your loved ones may feel guilty about cutting costs. And they may be overwhelmed by the number of decisions they'll need to make. Pre-planning your funeral is one of the best ways to avoid possible confusion over the type of arrangements you'd want and you may also save money.

The best way to pre-arrange a funeral is to sit down and talk with a trusted funeral director in your community. The Funeral Rule, enforced by the Federal Trade Commission, requires funeral directors to offer free consultations to give you advice, itemized prices and other information about their goods and services. Once you've made your pre-arrangements, keep a copy of your plan and any pertinent paperwork in a safe place. Also, inform a close friend or relative about the arrangements you have made and where the information can be found.

Pre-arranging your funeral doesn't require you to prepay for it. While I am a huge proponent of prearranging your funeral, I often tell people that before prepaying for a funeral, carefully evaluate the advantages and disadvantages listed on the next few pages.

The pros of prepaying for your funeral

Ability to choose the funeral home with the right personality

Your loved ones will be working with the funeral home staff at a very emotional and stressful time, so it's important that you choose a funeral home that you believe they'll be comfortable with.

Ability to comparison shop for prices and services

The costs of caskets and professional services vary dramatically. Obtain a detailed price list from the funeral homes you're considering, and take the time to compare your options to make an informed decision.

Protect against rising costs

Negotiate a contract that allows the purchase of tomorrow's merchandise and services at today's prices. This refers to an option you may have to pre-pay for your casket and funeral services. This cost protection guarantee, however, may not be as simple as it appears. Read the funeral service contract carefully, and if you're unsure about anything, ask questions. Also, each state has its own set of rules and regulations about how prepaid funeral expenses are handled. If you're unsure, call the state funeral directors association for more details. Choose a reputable funeral home and one with a long record of service to the community. If you don't know which funeral home to use, ask your friends and family for suggestions.

Reduce the size of the estate

Because this expense leaves less money in the bank, it means the size of the estate is a bit smaller. In some cases, this might result in less estate tax and/or may allow the individual to qualify for Medicaid benefits a touch sooner.

Shelter funds

If necessary, funds can be placed in an irrevocable trust for Medicaid or estate planning purposes.

Obtain peace of mind

Knowing that you'll be remembered exactly as you wish and ensuring that your loved ones won't be saddled with a heavy burden at a very vulnerable time will be a comfort to you today and as your time draws near.

The cons of prepaying for your funeral

Arrangements may not be portable

You may not be able to shift your arrangements to a new location if you leave the city you're currently living in. Have the funeral home explain in their contract the boundaries of their service area and under what circumstances you can transfer the pre-need contract to another funeral home if you were to relocate or if your death occurs outside of their service area.

Prices may not be guaranteed

If a funeral home didn't guarantee the prices of funeral costs and they inflate faster than the growth of the deposit, your loved ones will be forced to substitute less expensive merchandise or provide additional funding. Make sure the contract guarantees that if the merchandise or services selected aren't available at the time of need, merchandise or services of equal or greater value will be substituted at no extra cost.

If the prices aren't guaranteed, the contract should explain who will be responsible for paying any additional amounts that may be due at the time of the funeral. In the case of leftover funds, ensure that they'll be paid to your estate or else the funeral home will probably keep them.

Penalties may be lurking

If a prepaid funeral contract is cancelled, you may get back less than you paid. Not all states require funeral directors to provide a 100 percent refund. Furthermore, if payment is structured in installments and payments are not completed before your death, the refund may be reduced by a sales charge which could be as high as 30 percent. Make sure cancellation penalties and refund policies are spelled out in the contract.

Costs can be misunderstood

In many states, part or all of the interest earned on an account may be withdrawn each year by the seller as part of his administrative fees. Another typical misunderstanding is who will be responsible for paying taxes on the interest earned. Obtain a breakdown of all expenses in plain language and note in the contract who will be responsible for paying taxes on any income or interest generated by the invested funds.

The funeral home may not remain in business or it may get new owners

We are currently seeing a lot of changes in the funeral service industry. Small, family-owned businesses are closing and/or selling to larger national firms. Wholesale funeral homes, promising to save you thousands of dollars, are moving into many cities. A very real concern for anyone prepaying their arrangements is that the seller of those funeral services may not be in business at the time of your death or they may be under new ownership. Make sure that the pre-paid funds are secured and that the you or the account holder can withdraw them if the funeral home goes out of business or changes hands.

Your survivors may not know about the arrangements

The specifics of your pre-paid funeral must be made known to family members, otherwise that money can be lost. Make sure your funeral details are put in writing and a copy of the plan is kept in a safe place along with your other important papers. You should inform a family member, close friend or even your attorney that prearrangements have been made, who they have been made with and where the documents are kept.

Funding may be irrevocable

Before accepting an irrevocable agreement, carefully consider the implications of your decision. Irrevocable agreements are helpful when eligibility for Supplemental Security Income (SSI), Medicaid or other public benefits are being determined, but they may limit flexibility. Many states now offer you the option of designating funeral accounts as irrevocable at a later date, should this protection be necessary.

If Social Security benefits aren't a primary concern, consider using a Totten Trust. This is an individual trust or savings plan earmarked for one's funeral. The consumer controls the account and can withdraw from it at any time. Usually a sum of money equal to today's funeral costs is deposited in a passbook savings, Certificate of Deposit (CD) or money market account, payable to a beneficiary of the account holder's choice. These funds are available immediately at the time of death without the delay of probate. Accumulated interest helps cover costs increased by inflation.

Another alternative is life insurance with an increasing death benefit equal to the cost of the funeral. Funeral homes usually expect to be named the beneficiary, but that choice is up to you. Keep in mind, however, that the choice you make may determine whether or not the funeral home will freeze the costs at today's prices.

In summary, pre-paying a funeral is a nice gesture but caution should be taken. Maintaining control of the funds and/or making certain they are protected are considerations of paramount importance.

The National Funeral Directors Association—www.NFDA.org—is an excellent source of information on this topic or, better yet, sit down with a trusted funeral director and talk about the pros and cons that apply to your unique situation.

Appoint an Agent to Control Disposition of Your Remains

In some states, individuals are now able to legally assign an agent to control the disposition of their remains. Similar to a health care proxy or a living will, this legal document empowers the agent to make decisions on behalf of the individual—but specifically for taking care of the deceased's burial or cremation. In addition, the statute provides that an individual may give special directions, for example that they be cremated, that their body be buried in a particular grave at a specified cemetery, or that a particular funeral home handle the arrangements.

Appointing an agent to care for these matters is becoming popular for two reasons. First, even if a person's wishes are included in the will, an individual is usually buried or cremated long before a will is probated or even looked at. Second, with multiple marriages, same-sex relationships and individuals who are domestic partners, the disposition of a loved one's remains is increasingly being litigated. Be sure to check with your local funeral director for more details.

To-Do List

☐ Draft or modify your will as needed

☐ Draft a living will or health care proxy to make your wishes for life-prolonging treatment known

☐ Adopt a durable Power of Attorney

☐ Consider pre-arranging your funeral

☐ Identify beneficiaries/owners whenever possible on insurance policies, retirement accounts, etc.

☐ Consider putting individual accounts into jointly-held accounts

☐ Consider crafting or reviewing your current estate plan

☐ Appoint an agent to control the disposition of your remains

☐ _____

☐ _____

☐ _____

☐ _____

☐ _____

☐ _____

Notes

Chapter 11
Proactive Planning: Formalizing a Wisdom Will

As you know, dealing with the death of a loved one is complex. Not only do you have to navigate a maze of legal, financial and personal responsibilities, but you have to deal with your own emotions and grief.

One of the best ways you can help your loved ones when you die is to do some proactive planning now. Rather than leave them with unanswered questions, you can give them the information they need to get through the practical, legal, financial and personal matters they'll need to deal with after your death.

Your Wisdom Will

In addition to getting your legal will or trust in order, consider putting together a Wisdom Will. Your will or trust distributes your assets in an efficient manner. Your Wisdom Will, a companion to your will or trust, shares your wisdom in a meaningful way.

It can be hard to take the time and expend the emotional energy to think about the end of your life and what will be left behind when you die. But, creating a Wisdom Will actually gives you a lot of peace of mind, knowing you've taken the necessary steps to safeguard your loved ones from the confusion, conflict and despair that could otherwise follow your death. Plus, you'll have the comfort of knowing your last wishes will be heard and known, making it easy for your loved ones to carry them out.

It's comprised of four components: legal, practical, financial and personal.

Legal

You can help your loved ones understand the legal arrangements you've made, as well as the "why" behind the decisions in your legal will or trust. This insight could make the difference between family harmony and conflict.

Practical

In the aftermath of your death, you want your loved ones to be able to deal with matters in the easiest way possible. Taking care of this aspect of your life will prevent them from worrying about how you'd want things to be done, including your final wishes, where documents and passwords are located, how to care for pets and pay the bills.

Financial

You can provide advice on how you want your heirs to prudently handle finances. You, in turn, will find comfort and confidence knowing your loved ones will have the information they need as they navigate the financial challenges that often trouble people after a death.

Personal

By documenting family ancestry, memories and traditions, you know these things can live on.

You can also share your personal values, life lessons, thoughts on a family business or insight about your children for their guardians.

When to Create a Wisdom Will

While breaking the inertia of everyday living is often difficult, the uncertainty surrounding your date of death beckons a natural urgency. Also, you need to ask yourself what's worse: the thought of addressing the details surrounding your death or the consequences your loved ones would face if you don't?

For some people, a Wisdom Will can be completed in as little as an hour. Others might see it as a larger task and complete over the course of a few weeks. Either way, it's important to book the time in your calendar and, once started, don't lose momentum. Work on it consistently, a bit at a time until the plan is complete.

Creating Your Wisdom Will

Here are the steps to creating your own Wisdom Will document. You can create this as a document that you print and store with your other legal documents, or you can create it online at mywisdomwill.com.

Legal matters

The legal arrangements are all about determining who gets your stuff and how. It's a pretty basic concept but, with all of the moving parts, you'd be surprised how complicated it can get. To help your loved ones avoid confusion and frustration share your insight on any or all of the four matters below.

How your overall estate plan is designed

Explain the desired outcome of your estate plan and how it's constructed to accomplish that. When your loved ones know your objectives and how your estate plan is designed, they can better execute the desired steps.

Explain:

- How the estate plan is structured. Do you have a will, trust or other special arrangements?

- Who is responsible for what?

- What are your thoughts about charitable gifts and philanthropy?

Why it's designed that way

If your loved ones don't know why you made certain decisions, they have to guess at your intentions. This can cause pointless questioning and lead to family conflict.

Provide clarity around:

- Why did you structure you estate plan this way?

- Why did you chose certain people for their roles?

- Why are certain beneficiaries receiving an inheritance?

- Why are you giving money to charity, and why did you chose the charities you did?

Your business succession plan

If you own a business, share your high level overview for how you wish things to play out in your business. This doesn't replace your business succession plan.

Address matters such as:

- Short and long term vision
- Equity ownership
- Leadership and management
- Management suggestions
- Company culture
- Employee and/or family dynamics

Practical matters

Your loved ones will have enough to deal with after your death without worrying about where to find important paperwork or trying to figure out what you wanted.

Provide information for them on these practical topics.

Important people to contact after your death

Record contact information for the people you feel should be the first to know of your death and for important people who may be forgotten because of infrequent contact or long distance.

Your thoughts on your funeral/celebration of life

While the arrangements for your funeral, memorial service or celebration of life are often made according to the needs and wishes of your survivors, it's worthwhile to express your opinions. Your loved ones will usually want to honor your wishes, but that can be hard in the turmoil of grief if they don't know what they are.

Topics you can address include:

- Do you want a funeral, a memorial service or a celebration of life?

- Have you made any pre-arrangements? If so, where are they? Are they pre-paid?

- Do you have a preferred location or funeral home?

- Do you want to be buried or cremated? Do you have a preferred cemetery or crematorium?

- Would you like an obituary printed and, if so, what should it include?

- Are there any psalms, readings or songs you'd like at your service?

Organ donation and autopsy

In the minutes following your death, your loved ones need to be able to share your wishes about organ donation. Do you want some or all of your organs to be donated and where do you have formal documentation of these wishes?

Additionally, if there is uncertainty about the cause of your death, the question may arise about whether or not to do an autopsy. What are your thoughts and feelings on that? Perhaps you feel an autopsy is warranted if it benefits medical research, solves a crime or helps educate the medical field. Or perhaps you feel strongly that an autopsy should never be performed under any circumstances. Let your loved ones know.

Where you keep critical documents

Everyone has their own filing system that makes sense to them, but may not work for anyone else. After your passing, there are many crucial documents that your loved ones will need. Let them know where they can find each of the following documents. Common locations include a safe or filing cabinet at home, a bank safety deposit box, or with your attorney or financial advisor.

- Driver's license (or a photocopy)
- Passports
- Birth certificates/adoption papers
- Social Security card
- Service contracts
- Website access information
- Pet records
- Vaccination records
- Organ donor card
- Living will/healthcare proxy
- Durable power of attorney
- Stock/bond certificates
- Private loan papers

- Collectible coins, stamps, etc.
- Jewelry
- Trust agreement(s)
- Keys to safety deposit box
- Copy of your employee contract
- Pension plan records
- Tax returns
- Cost basis data
- Receipts for home improvements
- Marriage license
- Divorce decree(s)
- Prenuptial/postnuptial documents
- Deed(s) for home(s)
- Title(s) for auto(s)
- Deeds for other property
- Computer backup
- Credit cards
- Will
- Life insurance policies
- Disability insurance policies
- Long term care policies

- Death certificates
- Military papers
- Business agreements

Details about your online accounts

Our lives are increasingly lived online, especially our financial lives. Your loved ones will need to know how to access your online accounts or they may experience frustration and financial mishaps.

Educate your loved ones about:

- Online accounts—which ones you have and for what purpose, including email, social networks, blogging sites, photo sharing sites, frequent flier accounts, shopping sites such as Amazon.com and eBay, credit card accounts, bank accounts and online bill payment accounts such as the ones you have for your utilities.

- Passwords—where they are or the strategy you use to create and remember them, as well as the answers to your security questions.

- Email—your email accounts and how to handle them.

189

- Social media—your accounts and how to handle them. Should your loved ones keep them open in your legacy or close them?

- Digital assets—what digital assets you own, including video games, movies and music, and what you want your loved ones to do with them.

Household maintenance tips

If your surviving loved ones aren't familiar with how to maintain the household, leave them guidance. Consider topics such as:

- Technicians you trust for auto, plumbing, electrical, lawn, etc.

- Existing service contracts you have on appliances, furnace, etc.

- Seasonal chores that aren't obvious, e.g. cleaning a particular rain gutter.

Insight about caring for children and adult dependents

This information is intended to be shared with caretakers, guardians and trustees of your surviving minor children and adult dependents. Don't dictate how to raise the children or care for your elderly parents. However, you can share guidance to empower their caretakers or guardians to continue providing quality care.

Contact information for doctors and other medical providers, allergies and medical needs, and special care instructions can all be helpful. Behavioral observations are also important as they can help the caretaker handle things in a more meaningful and effective way.

Instructions on how to care for your pets

Your beloved pet(s) will have a new caretaker. This is your opportunity to share anything that might make the transition easier. Your wisdom will also go a long way to ensure your pet(s) receive the care they deserve. Document information about your pet's:

- Daily care instructions
- Food, allergies and medication
- Any medical conditions
- Behavioral conditions
- Veterinarian

- Caretakers that might be able to help care for your pet(s) or adopt them

Medical history that could impact your survivors

Family have many factors in common, including their genes, environment and lifestyle. Together, these factors can give clues to medical conditions that may run in a family.

By noticing patterns of disorders among relatives, healthcare professionals can determine whether an individual, other family members or future generations may be at increased risk of developing a particular condition.

For these reasons, share any notable medical history that might be beneficial for your loved ones and future generations to be aware of.

Financial matters

Have peace of mind knowing you've safeguarded your loved ones from the financial despair that often plagues families after a death. Share your insight with your loved ones on these seven matters.

Overall state of finances and philosophies on money management

Give a high level overview of your finances, with just enough information to bring your survivors up to speed with the general health of your finances and how you have chosen to manage them. You can also share your wisdom about how they can prudently manage money. Although your surviving loved ones may have their own approach, they might find your wisdom informative and helpful.

How your trusted financial advisor(s) can lend a hand

If you have a relationship with one or more financial advisors, share their contact information, the dynamics of your relationship and an explanation of how they might be of assistance to your loved ones.

A list of savings, assets and liabilities

Provide your loved ones detailed information about the amount and location of savings and investments as well as assets and liabilities. Also list any personal debt obligations to be paid or received.

If you have this your assets and liabilities documented somewhere already, let your survivors know where that is.

The practice of paying bills and managing debt

Do you have any personal financial debts that need to be repaid? Or other bills your survivors may not know about? Personal IOUs and other informal arrangements are common. Identifying them will help your survivors make sure that such obligations are satisfied.

Details about death benefits from your life insurance

What are all the potential sources of life insurance your survivors can collect? You may have traditional term or whole life insurance, but don't forget life insurance policies through your employer, union, credit card, mortgage provider, bank, university, etc.

List the insurance amounts, carriers and agent information, or where your survivors can find this information.

The monetary death benefit provided by your life insurance can help in various ways. It might be a means of replacing lost income, paying estate taxes, covering the cost of college, paying off debts, etc. Provide some insight as to how you envisioned your life insurance benefit would help your loved ones.

Death benefits in addition to life insurance that your beneficiaries should collect

Beyond life insurance, your survivors might be eligible to collect other death benefits that provide a lump-sum or income stream. This is not where you would list accumulated savings. Rather, this is for contractual benefits that are only paid upon your death.

They may come from:

- Social security and veteran benefits
- Pension plans
- Tax-deferred annuity

Income tax highlights that might save your survivors money

If you have an accountant then they are likely to know most or all of the information necessary to prudently manage your taxes. In such case you can list their name and a brief description of your relationship.

If you don't have an accountant or would like to share additional information, then list it here. Examples include location of cost basis data, estimated tax projections, typical tax withholdings, RMD rules, tips on how to minimize taxes, whether or not the taxes are paid electronically (via online accounts), etc.

Personal matters

You matter. Share with the world who you are and what you stand for. This information can have a profound impact on the lives of future generations and is too valuable to risk being lost. Below are seven things to consider writing about.

Your personal values and/or principals

This is your opportunity to shape the legacy for which you will be remembered. Share your perspective on what's important in life—your personal values and guiding principles. Unlike your physical property that can decay, disappear or become extinct, your values can live forever. To cultivate some ideas, here are some questions to ponder:

- What is really important to you?
- What have you done in life to stand up for you values?
- How do you define true success?
- What does spirituality mean to you?

In your own life, you'll discover that the clearer your values become, the easier it is to make decisions about how to spend your time.

The lessons you have learned in your lifetime

Along the journey of life you've learned invaluable lessons. If you have life lessons that have influenced the way you live your life then record them here. It's a wonderful opportunity to positively impact future generations. To stimulate your thinking ask yourself:

- Has there been an event (or person) that changed your life and why?

- Are there any interesting or funny stories?

- Are there accomplishments or actions you're proud of?

- What are some things you have learned about love and relationships?

- What are some things you have learned about dealing with challenges and/or opportunities?

Special instructions regarding personal possessions of emotional value

Very often, personal possessions of emotional value are treasured by loved ones more than material goods and money. These are items such as photographs, family recipes, an old baseball glove, collectibles, a hand-made cookie plate, etc. Because each item has a unique meaning, it might be best to let your loved ones choose who gets what. Nonetheless, if you would like to make suggestions or gift a certain item to a particular person then feel free to express your desires.

Cherished traditions that celebrate the uniqueness of your family or culture

Traditions are a valuable way to strengthen families, remind of us our heritage and create lasting memories. New or old, share any traditions that you would like embraced by future generations.

Your family history is an important part of who you are

Knowing where you came from is a magical story that does more than satisfy curiosity. It helps you identify with who you are culturally and spiritually. Share a high-level overview of your family history and, if applicable, tell loved ones where they can go to obtain more information. If you have already obtained research through one of the many online ancestry services be sure to leave login credentials.

Meaningful stories and memories

Record, share and preserve the stories of your life to strengthen and build the connections with your loved ones and future generations. Whether it be from childhood or today or whether it's funny, sad, serious or silly, your story matters. To take it a step further consider visiting www.storycorps.org to learn about how you can vocally record your stories and have them preserved in the archive at the Library of Congress!

Leave your legacy letter

In the format of a personal letter, write whatever you'd like to share with your loved ones. Whether it be life lessons, principles, or emotions. Share your blessings and speak from the heart.

To get inspired, read Barack Obama's legacy letter to his daughters and Richard Branson's "Letter to my Grandchildren." They are easily found by searching the internet.

Who would you like your "messenger(s)" to be?

Determine one of more people who you trust to share your Wisdom Will and, if necessary, assist in carrying out your wishes.

Live with Purpose

Create a "bucket list" of goals you would like to accomplish before you "kick the bucket." It will inspire you as you move forward with your life. Include things you've always dreamt of doing, as well as short-term goals like becoming more organized. Keep your list current by adding, editing or marking complete any item on your list.

Imagine the impact you could have on future generations. You could inspire your great-grandchild to accomplish the same things that you did. Who knows, you might start a family tradition of climbing the high peaks in the Adirondack Mountains or visiting underdeveloped countries to help humankind.

Notes

Afterword

When Joanne died, I put my life on hold. For many months, life was consumed with the day-to-day details of her death. But slowly, I went back to work, began arranging social engagements and eventually introduced new people and new activities into my life, while still remaining close to Joanne's family and friends. When daily routine set in, the structure was a welcome relief. I will never forget Joanne, but I have learned how to continue on with my life in a positive and life-affirming way.

After dealing with my grief and learning to adapt to a life different than the one I had hoped for, I have created a new life for myself. In 2003, I married Kathy, a wonderful woman who has brought light, laughter and a world of possibilities to my life. I am proud to announce that I also have been blessed with two beautiful children, my son Christopher and daughter Emily.

So, my final message to you is one of inspiration. Remember that while life may bring us unfair challenges from time to time, it can also bring un-expected blessings we never dreamed of.

Additional Resources

The following resources provide more information on various topics discussed throughout this book. To be sure of current numbers and addresses, please check the Internet.

American Bar Association
www.abanet.org

Career Gear (donations of men's clothing)
www.CareerGear.org

Department of Veterans Affairs

800-827-1000 or www.va.gov

Do Not Call Registry
www.donotcall.gov

Dress for Success (donations of women's clothing)
www.DressforSuccess.org

Federal Trade Commission's ID Theft Hotline
877-438-4338 or www.consumer.gov/idtheft

Fraud Insurance

www.identityfraud.com or
www.javelinstrategy.com

Funeral Consumers Alliance

www.funerals.org or 800-765-0107

Funeral Consumers Alliance is a nonprofit organization dedicated to protecting a consumer's right to choose a meaningful, dignified and affordable funeral.

Gift of Life Donation Initiative

www.organdonor.gov

The Grief Recovery Institute

818-907-9600 or www.grief.net

The Grief Recovery Institute offers an action program for moving beyond loss and a great series of articles that can help you get a clearer picture of what is true and accurate in relationship to both grief and recovery.

Internal Revenue Service

800-829-1040 or www.IRS.gov

Mark Colgan, CFP®

585-419-2270 or

www.montagewm.com or
www.mywisdomwill.com
Founding Partner, Montage Wealth Management,
and Creator, www.mywisdomwill.com.

National Funeral Directors Association

414-541-2500 or www.NFDA.org

National Self-Help Clearinghouse

(212) 840-1259
Provides information on variety of peer support
groups.

Social Security Administration

800-772-1213 or 800-325-0778 TTY or
www.SSA.gov

Glossary

Administrator

A person appointed by the court to supervise the handling of an individual's estate in the event that no will has been executed.

Affidavit

Any written document in which the signer swears under oath before a notary public or someone authorized to take oaths (like a County Clerk), that the statements in the document are true.

Beneficiary

The named party who receives proceeds under an insurance policy, trust or will.

Bond

A debt security, similar to an IOU When you purchase a bond, you're lending money to a government, municipality, corporation, federal agency, or other entity known as the issuer.

Cash Value

The "savings element" in a permanent life insurance policy, which is the property of the policy owner.

Certificate of Deposit

A deposit with a specified maturity date and interest rate.

Certified Financial Planner™

Anyone can call themselves a financial planner, but only those individuals who have voluntarily taken the extra step to demonstrate their professionalism and high ethical standards can be certified by the Certified Financial Planner Board of Standards. Their accreditation indicates they are capable in financial planning as well as managing a client's banking, estate, insurance, investment and tax affairs. Only those individuals can call themselves a Certified Financial Planner and use the CFP designation after their name.

Codicil

A document that amends a will. It must be executed

like a will and witnessed by two people not named as beneficiaries for any of the assets.

Creditor

Lender of monies.

Death Benefit

The proceeds of the policy that will be paid upon insured's death.

Decedent

A person who has died. Also referred to as the deceased.

Dependent parent

A parent who is determined to be dependent under IRS standards and for whom an exemption can be claimed. See IRS Publication 501 for more information.

Disclaimer

The refusal, rejection or renunciation of a claim, power or property.

Estate Tax

A tax paid on property or assets owned at the time of death.

Executor/Executrix

An individual appointed through a will to administer and distribute property upon the testator's death. Executor is the male version and executrix is the female form of the word.

Fiduciary

An individual who manages property or acts on behalf of another individual and is placed in a position of trust.

Guardian

An individual who has the legal right and duty to take care of another person or another's property because that person cannot legally handle these responsibilities.

Health Care Proxy (Health Care Power of Attorney)

A legal document that allows you to appoint someone to make medical decisions if you become unable to competently make them for yourself.

Interment

The act of burial.

Individual Retirement Account (IRA)

A retirement account that may have been established by an employed or self-employed individual.

IRA Rollover

A provision enabling a retiree or anyone receiving a lump-sum payment from pension, profit-sharing or salary reduction plan to transfer the amount into an IRA.

IRA Beneficiary Distribution Account (IRA-BDA)

A retirement account established by a beneficiary. An inheritance where the deceased's name remains on the account.

Intestate or Intestacy

The state of dying without a legal will where a probate court oversees asset distribution.

Irrevocable

Unable to be amended, altered or revoked.

Legacy

A combination of life facts, photos, video clips, favorite stories, powerful memories and wisdom that one can package together as a gift to future generations of one's family.

Medicaid

A joint federal and state program that helps with medical costs for people with low incomes and limited resources.

Medicare

The federal health insurance program for people 65 years and older. Certain people who are younger but who have disabilities and/or serious illness may also be eligible.

Living Trust

A legal arrangement, established during an individual's lifetime and which is fully amendable and revocable by its creator, under which a trustee holds title to property with the obligation to keep or use it for the benefit of the beneficiary. Living Trusts are commonly used as vehicles to avoid probate.

Living Will

A legal document allowing you to express your wishes as to health care treatment, not estate planning. It makes clear what measures you want taken—or not taken—to keep you alive if you're seriously ill.

Mutual Fund

A financial intermediary that allows a group of investor to pool their money together under a fund manager who buys and sells securities with a predetermined investment objective.

Power of Attorney

A document that authorizes someone to act on another's behalf.

Power of Appointment

Typically used with trusts, it gives an individual the power to decide which beneficiaries receive distributions and in what amounts.

Principal

The total amount of money being borrowed or lent.

Probate

The process of proving that a will is genuine and distributing the property accordingly.

Roth IRA

A type of individual retirement account that allows contributors to make annual contributions and to withdraw the principal and earnings tax-free under certain conditions.

Stock Certificate

A document reflecting legal ownership of a specific number of stock shares in a corporation.

Testamentary Trust

A trust that is created upon the death of the decedent pursuant to the terms of the will through or as a result of the probate process.

Trust

A legal arrangement in which an individual holds title to property, subject to an obligation to keep or use it for the benefit of the beneficiary.

Trustee

A person who holds money or property for the benefit of another.

Supplemental Security Income (SSI)

Monthly benefits paid by the Social Security Administration to individuals who qualify because of limited income and resources or who are disabled, blind or age 65 or older.

Surrogate's Court

County or state court that handles cases involving the affairs of decedents, including administration of wills, estates and trusts.

Transfer Agent

Individual or institution that a company appoints to handle the ownership transfer of securities.

Transfer on Death (TOD)

The process of changing the title of a security from one name to another upon the death of one of the titleholders.

Urn

Container designed to hold an individual's cremated remains.

Will

A legal document through which a person declares or designates how their possessions will pass after death.

Index

Index

How to Order More Books

If you found the knowledge, insight and experience in *Details After Death* helpful, perhaps you'd like to share the information with a friend, business associate or family member. Or pass the word to your doctors, hospice nurse, religious leader, funeral director, social worker, therapist and support group.

Call: 585-419-2270

Write: Mark Colgan
179 Sully's Trail, Suite 302
Pittsford, NY 14534

Online: www.mywisdomwill.com

About the Author

Having experienced the unexpected death of his beloved wife, Joanne, Mark learned at the early age of 31 the fragility of life and the importance of proper planning. A bitter-sweet yet valuable life experience, it helped cultivate his success as a comprehensive and compassionate Wealth Manager.

His Role as a Wealth Manager

Mark's goal isn't just to help clients maximize the return on their investments; it's also to maximize how the returns can make a difference in their life. A goal inspired by his fundamental belief that while money can't buy happiness, when prudently managed, it can support your efforts to achieve your personal goals that contribute to your happiness.

Additionally, Mark has a niche expertise in helping widows and widowers. Once a widower himself, he understands the unique financial needs and overwhelming emotional challenges they face in the midst of losing a loved one. This personal vantage, combined with his wealth management expertise, uniquely positions him to help widows and widowers build a secure foundation for a more promising future.

Extensive Credentials

Mark Colgan has been in the financial services industry for two decades. Prior to his career, Mark earned his BS in finance from the Rochester Institute of Technology.

- CFP® practitioner
- FINRA Series 7 registration (General Securities Representative)*

- FINRA Series 63 registration (Uniform Securities Agent State Law)*

- FINRA Series 65 registration (Uniform Investment Adviser Law)*

- Life and Health Insurance licenses

- Registered Representative and Investment Adviser Representative of Commonwealth Financial Network®, the largest privately held independent broker/dealer in the nation, to take advantage of all the services and resources they offer

A Cited Expert

- Nationally recognized specialist on the topic of legacy planning

- Author of *Details After Death*, a fifth edition of *The Survivor Assistance Handbook*

- Articles published in *U.S. News and World Report*, the *Journal of Financial Planning*, *American Association of Individual Investors*, and *Money Adviser*, a consumer reports publication

- Previously cited by FOX News, CBS MarketWatch, Oprah and Friends, Morningstar.com, and other mainstream media

On a Personal Note

Mark resides in the countryside just outside of Rochester, New York. He also enjoys spending his free time in the Adirondack Mountains with his beautiful wife, two children, and Labradors.

About the Author

63322682R00150

Made in the USA
Lexington, KY
04 May 2017